PARENTING WELL AFTER CHILDHOOD ABUSE

Be a Great Parent
Even if Yours Were Crap

Geanne Meta

Copyright © 2019 by Geanne Meta. All rights reserved.

No part of this publication may be reproduced, distributed, or transmitted in any form or by any means, including photocopying, recording, or other electronic or mechanical methods, without the prior written permission of the publisher, except in the case of brief quotations embodied in reviews and certain other non-commercial uses permitted by copyright law.

ISBN-13: 978-1-7332513-1-0

Extra! Extra!

Go to
https://Mailchi.mp/69aa1689ab86/parentingwaca

<u>To get free downloads of</u>:

Worksheet: "Connect With Your Inner Child"

Questionnaire: "What You Want to Do Differently Than Your Parents"

"10 Things to Discuss Before Having Kids"

Group Discussion or Individual Work Guide

For my soul sister, Terrin.
This book would not be possible
without your love and support.
Your honesty helped me to live in truth.
Your strength and courage came first
and guided me to healing.
I am grateful beyond measure for you in my life.

For Sierra and Devin
You are the treasures of my life.
You changed everything,
making it possible for me to become my best self.

For some family members who haven't heard my story,
I hope this brings clarity and understanding.

Table of Contents

Introduction

PART 1 – HEALING YOURSELF

Chapter 1: Breaking the Cycle of Abuse	7
Chapter 2: Why Go to Therapy?	15
Chapter 3: Recognizing Denial	25
Chapter 4: Setting Boundaries	37
Chapter 5: Learning to Be Kind to Yourself	43
Chapter 6: Relationships and Divorce	51
Chapter 7: Forgiveness	65

PART 2 – RAISING GOOD KIDS

Introduction	75
Chapter 1: Children's Bill of Rights	79
Chapter 2: Honesty is the Best Policy	83
Chapter 3: The Power of Apology	87
Chapter 4: Managing Expectations. Accepting Feelings	93
Chapter 5: Who's in Charge?	103
Chapter 6: Random Parenting Advice	111

Chapter 7: Child Safety	125
Chapter 8: Dealing with Teenagers	137
Conclusion	145
Recommended Reading	147
Resources	149
Acknowledgements	151
About the Author	153
Group Discussion - Individual Work Guide	157

Introduction

Parenting is hard. You are presented with even more struggles when you were harmed by your parents as a child. There are deep wounds that need to be healed. You should seek guidance and inspiration wherever you can. The fact that you picked up this book shows that you want to change unhealthy patterns and be a better parent than yours were.

I am a survivor of childhood sexual abuse. My father molested me from a young age and my mother looked the other way. I started drinking alcohol when I was 12 years old. I had self-destructive behaviors, abusing drugs and alcohol for years. I struggled with anger, depression, anxiety and poor self-esteem. But I didn't seek help until I became a parent. That's when everything changed. It was time to take care of myself because I needed to be my best for the innocent child that I was blessed with.

Everyone's healing journey is unique. Yours will not be the same as mine. Survivors of sexual, physical and/or emotional abuse share many of the same struggles caused by the trauma. You can gain perspective and hope from hearing my story.

My journey is here to help guide you through yours. I wish that I had started sooner. I wish I had had more support. But everything happens in its own time and we must be gentle with ourselves. Unfortunately, you cannot rush the healing process.

As a child you learned to cope and survive in ways that may have become habits. You may have learned to shut down, be fearful, aggressive, anxious, depressed, or self-loathing. As an adult, these scars don't automatically go away. Invisible wounds exist that need to heal.

If you had one instance of molestation, it can wreck how you think of yourself from that moment on. Until you get help to see things differently, the old patterns can really become stuck. There are layers of pain to get through. The freedom from shame and the benefits of becoming truly happy are worth it. You and your children are worth the effort.

There are many kinds of child abuse and they are all harmful to developing brains, hearts and bodies. Parents can be alcoholics or drug addicts. They can be physically, sexually, and emotionally abusive; or cold, absent and neglectful of your needs.

Though some people suffered horrific abuse and others were abandoned, your pain and feelings about your situation are valid. If you were neglected and told that you were garbage, maybe literally put into a garbage can, as an adult you may think that it wasn't so bad; and you're over it. When you realize how harmful that was to a small child you can begin to heal it. This book will help you get out of denial so you can realize what your inner child needs.

If you haven't looked at what happened and understood how your young-self processed it – it's probably still affecting how you live your life.

You could understandably lack self-confidence and the motivation to try harder. You may have terrible self-talk and not trust anyone who says they love you. You must address the shame, self-blame, denial, unhealthy coping, anger, depression, and low self-esteem. It's difficult to fix these things without help.

That's the main message here – to seek help to break the cycle of abuse. Find counseling, support groups, God, self-help

INTRODUCTION

books or anything else that works for you at the time. This book will give you direction and motivation to stop old belief patterns you may have about yourself so you can start healing.

The abuse happened and I'm trying to use the experience to help others to heal as I have. Making something positive out of the negative only makes sense.

My abuse colored everything. Even though some of my self-doubt and feelings of inadequacy are normal, I see myself through the filter of abuse. It's in this context that I describe my parenting and healing challenges throughout this book.

Healing will allow you to grow and stop feeling stunted. Don't wait another minute to start. Your kids are only small for a short time and they are depending on you.

PART 1

HEALING YOURSELF

"When you know better, you do better"
—Maya Angelou

Chapter 1

Breaking the Cycle of Abuse

Of course, you know it's important to break the cycle of abuse. It stops with you when you decide to take steps to stop it. But exactly what does this mean?

You want to be a good parent. You don't want to damage your kids the way that you were harmed. You must see your childhood realistically and then decide to take steps to break the cycle. You must heal yourself to be the best parent you can be for your children.

I chose to cut my father from my baby's life because I didn't want to be worried about her safety around him. I didn't want to be hyper-vigilant if he were around. It was such a relief once I told him that there wouldn't be any contact between us unless I initiated it. I had no contact for 14 years. I made this decision because of my children. I had not considered it for myself before.

My mother's death, 6 weeks after my daughter was born, freed me to be able to cut contact with my father. It was for her that I had kept up the pretense that our family was normal.

My kids grew up without grandparents on my side, but it was much better that way. Besides the safety issues, I may not have been able to break out of the emotional shackles if I had continued interacting with my father. Once I went to therapy, told my story and felt acceptance for it, I simply couldn't go back to pretending everything was fine.

I was setting boundaries and breaking the cycle of abuse.

But it takes more than being hyper-vigilant to protect your kids from harm. You must become emotionally healthy to meet the challenges of parenting. Changing patterns of behavior doesn't happen automatically because you have the desire to change. You will need help. You must learn healthier ways to treat yourself and find the courage to heal.

You can learn to break free of the dysfunctional ways your family of origin operated. This includes getting out of denial, setting boundaries, having safety rules, being honest and learning to love yourself. The next few chapters will go into more detail on these topics.

Feeling Not Good Enough

At a young age you were forming opinions about yourself and what was happening in your family. Because of how you were treated, you probably jumped to a conclusion that may or may not have been true.

A common belief you may have formed is: I'm not good enough.

Why? 1) Because you didn't make the grades that were expected? 2) Because you weren't very good at baseball? 3) Because you were clumsy and fell down a lot? 4) Because someone told you that?

BREAKING THE CYCLE OF ABUSE

You can find opposite reasons for all of the above examples. 1) Straight A's are a goal – not a realistic expectation. 2) I bet you were good at other things. 3) Maybe you had an inner ear problem. 4) it's possible that your parent was a very troubled person who needed to get help.

The book <u>"Loving What Is: Four Questions That Can Change Your Life"</u> by Byron Katie helped me learn how to change my negative thinking. I was stuck with the same thoughts about myself and others in my life. Believing what you're thinking can be a negative cycle. You can learn to challenge those thoughts and see things in a much more positive way.

One day I realized my habit of automatically calling myself a name. I reached to get a cup from the cupboard, it slipped, fell to the floor and I immediately thought "You stupid idiot." My inner voice jolted me. I realized that this was my go-to name for myself. I thought "Wow. Where did that come from? I am not a stupid idiot because the cup fell."

Accidents happen all the time. As adults we usually cuss and move on. Can we please practice this same kind of forgiveness for all the mistakes of our children? Learn to become aware of your self-talk and be gentle with yourself. Change it or you most certainly will pass it on to your children.

A common insecurity that most humans have is the feeling that they aren't good enough. Enough already. We can't all be stupid idiots. Where does this come from?

It comes from when you were a child and you knew nothing of the world. You were dependent on your parents. You came into the world as a perfect soul, full of unlimited potential. Everyone agreed that you were a beautiful baby, you were so cute. Everything you did was awesome and a picture opportunity to be posted somewhere.

As soon as you started getting around on your own – you made mistakes and were told "No, No". You formed opinions about yourself from that moment on. You thought, "Oh, mommy and daddy love me when I'm a certain way, but they frown and tell me no when I'm unhappy or touch something."

It's normal for children to be self-centered and believe that the world revolves around them. It's natural for them to think that they are bad or good from our reactions. Parents must try to give more positive praise and encouragement than negative statements. Life will throw plenty of negatives the kid's way.

What does a good parent look like?

Before having a child; it would be nice if everyone were in the perfect place in their life, with the right partner, ready and emotionally capable of being a parent. That doesn't always happen. Let's face it, almost anyone who can have sex can become a parent. If people were mature and prepared for parenthood perhaps there would be less abuse and neglect.

In this life, you take what you get and work with it. Maybe our parents did the best they could with what they were given. They may have just been continuing the cycle of what was done to them. However, that is not an excuse for mistreating their children.

Breaking the cycle means taking time to really think about what kind of parent you want to be. Realize that your parents had shortcomings and so will you. You're only human after all. But that doesn't mean that you can't do better. Much better.

Start by seeking help and learn to see your children as gifts to the earth. You're just their caretaker for a while. They are not possessions, slaves or reflections of you. Their job is not to please you or make you happy. You have to find your happiness from within. If you are unhappy, it's time to work on that so you can be there for your kids.

While I worked to become a better parent I had to break ties with my father in order to protect my child (and future child). I also made sure to have a loving home, fostering closeness and trust with my children. I had to realize what I had needed as a child and give it to my kids.

Breaking the cycle of blaming yourself

First, it's important that you challenge how you think about yourself and what happened to you. When a child is abused by a parent or other adult, they can blame themselves. You probably learned to deny and downplay the actions of your abuser.

To move forward as a parent, it's important for you to find compassion and love for yourself. It may take some work to really understand that whatever treatment you got as a child was not your fault. You deserved to be taken care of and loved.

It's possible to reparent yourself right along with parenting your own precious child, to find joy and laughter in the small moments, to realize that you are capable and strong. Try to see yourself as your baby sees you – with love and adoration.

It's important to break the cycle of negative thoughts and feelings that you formed about yourself.

I was raised with the feeling that I was bad, and my parents' unhappiness was my fault, so I had to work very hard to change those thoughts. I was used to believing negative things about myself. Even when people would give me compliments, I didn't accept their flattery. I thought if they only knew what was inside of me, they wouldn't like me. I believed that my parents hated me, which was a bitter pill and deeply wounding. Does this sound familiar?

Even when my parents were nice and did things for me, I didn't trust their motives. I remembered my father's perversion and my mother's cold distance from me. The abuse overshadowed everything on a subconscious level.

When I finally escaped hell and left home, I realized I had no idea how to help myself and wasn't aware of any resources to help me. I relied on my best friend and my sister, who was also abused by our father; to show me what love was and that I wasn't crazy. Home was an insane situation that had nothing to do with how lovable, good or bad I was.

Although I acknowledged the abuse, it wasn't until I went to therapy that I began to see the situation clearly and was able to start the healing. I had to break the cycles of denial, anger and negative self-talk to become a whole person. It took a while to learn to love and respect myself.

When you remember yourself as a child and realize your innocence, you can begin to break the cycle of shame and self-blame. You can learn to give love to yourself. When you can treat your inner child with kindness, you're on your way to healing your wounds from childhood.

By working on self-acceptance, you'll be better able to treat your own children with gentleness and compassion. If you aren't emotionally healthy, you run the risk of continuing the cycle.

Think about how you were treated as a child. Were your needs taken care of, were you a slave, did you have rights or respect? Did anyone apologize for their actions? How do you wish it had been different?

Parenting is learned behavior. You have some natural instincts to love your infant but as soon as the crap hits the fan and you want to stop them from ruining your day, you often resort back to yelling or losing your mind as your parent(s) did.

Correcting learned behavior doesn't happen automatically. Working to understand your feelings will help you to break this cycle of behavior.

My mother unhappily stayed home while my father worked. She yelled at us often and didn't want us to play in the house. She yelled about our rooms being messy, if we used too much toilet paper, if we drank her Sprite and to get out of her sight. I didn't want to be like her when I had kids. However, I found myself getting angry when mine would disobey me and sometimes couldn't control my yelling. I had to work to break this cycle.

The number one thing you must do is to GET HELP as soon as possible.

Learn new ways to deal with your feelings. Get some counseling. I believe everyone on the planet can use therapy at some time in their life. It may not seem possible when you have a young family. But the time and money will be well spent to get you on the right track to healing.

If it's hard to get in touch with your inner child, then take some time to observe your own child with love. Should they have a care in the world? Should they be protected from harm and any drama in your world right now? What do they need? Can you rise to the challenge to be a better parent than yours were?

PARENTING WELL AFTER CHILDHOOD ABUSE

The hope is that each generation will try to do better for their family, that's evolution for you. You probably want to leap ahead and heal yourself so that you don't just do a little better but completely break the cycle. Be kind to yourself and realize that changes are going to take some time.

Change may also be threatening to your parents and siblings. Realize you can't change them, just yourself. Change will be especially hard if you have a lot of contact with your family. Part of the problem is that dysfunctional families don't want to see anyone alter the "old way" of doing things.

It's your decision to heal and don't expect others to understand or support you right away. You can only live by example.

Breaking the cycle is what it's all about. It's possible and very well worth it. If only one person from every abusive family can break the cycle rather than pass it on to the next generation, then our human society could be healed and fully functional - in about a thousand years. Just imagine if this were possible. It can begin with you.

You will need help. The next chapter explores why you should see a professional.

Vulnerability is the bravest space
When you put yourself in the light, no one can hurt you
Put the pain and shame in the light
and it's no longer hidden, painful or shameful
Be unapologetic for taking care of your needs
Listen to your authentic voice
Trust it

Chapter 2

Why Go to Therapy?

If you had a gaping, bleeding and painful wound you would go straight to a doctor, right? Just because your childhood wounds aren't visible doesn't mean that they don't need attention. The pain's there and likely to show up in the ways you act around your children. It runs deep inside you and it's OK to ask for help. In fact, for an abuse victim to become a survivor, it's absolutely necessary to see a professional who can help you move forward.

Although you may have been living your life without thinking of your abuse, you probably felt an underlying sadness and a great divide between yourself and others. You deserve to live a happy life. Give yourself the love and respect that you didn't receive as a child.

You'll need to find a good counselor or talk to a trusted clergy. Once things from your childhood come up it's important not to bury them or let them go back into hiding. The main thing to realize is that you weren't responsible for anything that happened. You were supposed to be protected and nurtured.

I looked like an adult on the outside but felt like a wounded child a lot of the time on the inside. I felt out of control of my emotions and anger. I never felt like an equal partner in relationships. I had fears of abandonment and of being controlled. My inner child was running my emotional life and she was ill-equipped.

I needed to get in touch with my deep feelings and learn new ways to cope. I needed help to shed light on my past and see it in a realistic way.

You may be thinking, I know what happened to me. I understand that I was abused, neglected, abandoned and hurt by adults who were supposed to care for me. What good will it do to talk about it over and over?

This is adult, rational thinking.

These are thoughts in your head.

What is hurting you are the feelings that got stuck, buried, stomped on when you were very young. You need to get to those feelings of your inner child and heal them once and for all. It's very hard to do on your own.

You may tell yourself "It wasn't that bad, I got through it OK."

Yes, you survived. But your mind and heart have put up protective barriers. Denial is a strong force to be reckoned with. The reason, I hope, you picked up this book is because you know that there's more to it. Figuring that out begins with therapy.

A therapist is trained to help you realize what you cannot see for yourself. They also have techniques and homework to help you heal. You may not be aware of the many ways the abuse has affected you.

It can make you feel a lot less crazy to understand why you react to some things out of proportion to the event. You may not have identified where your intense feelings of anger, mistrust, sadness and your control issues come from. I know that I hadn't. I was blaming everyone else for my reactions. Partners didn't behave how I wanted them to.

WHY GO TO THERAPY?

It's worth looking into what resources there are in your community. I found my first therapist through Jewish Family Services in my town, although I'm not Jewish. My second therapist was reasonably priced, and I saw her for three years.

I've been blessed over the years to have found what I needed from therapists and groups at the right times. I've gone to therapy off and on for a total of 10 years. Sometimes it was necessary to take breaks and then life showed me that I needed to do some more work. Everyone's road to healing is their own to travel. But you can find support to help you.

In addition to finding a good therapist, there are plenty of self-help avenues to explore. Find books on parenting that speak to you. You can learn yoga, meditate or do your own healing exercises to try to learn to calm and control your anger.

Therapy is hard. Especially at first. My first husband told me that he didn't think it was helping me because I was crying all the time. But I had years of pent up emotions and the first one that spurted out was sadness. People around you may not know how to help, and it's not always easy to tell them what you need. Try asking for hugs and the words "I'm sorry for your pain."

It's not easy to lift the veil of secrecy. It hurts, but not any worse than what you have already been feeling. It will get better. There is hope and healing on the other side.

Even though through therapy you must relive some of the pain for the healing to start, it's a necessary part of the process. You've been living with pain anyway.

Therapy starts a grieving process. You'll realize that you didn't get the childhood that you deserved or the parents that you wanted, and must grieve that.

PARENTING WELL AFTER CHILDHOOD ABUSE

Elisabeth Kubler-Ross devised a framework for grief's 5 stages:

1. Denial and Isolation
2. Anger
3. Bargaining
4. Depression
5. Acceptance

You may go through them in a different order or not experience all of them, but you will find yourself feeling some of these stages when you embrace the process.

I know that I was stuck in anger for a long time. Once I put the blame squarely on my parents for not protecting me and neglecting my feelings, I was angry with them. It felt good. I didn't have to be angry at myself any more. I also learned not to be so angry at the other people in my life when they didn't meet my emotional needs.

My eyes were opened to how my parents mistreated me and the fact that I didn't deserve it. My heart was opened to love myself – and the little girl (my inner child) that I had neglected. Before therapy I had blamed myself, discounting my inner child's feelings, her needs for love and understanding.

Therapy reinforced for me that what had happened to me was terrible and hurtful to my soul. Speaking about it helped me to see the situation in a new light. I wasn't shamed or made to feel badly about what happened to me - quite the opposite; I was believed and supported. I wish this for all of you.

WHY GO TO THERAPY?

Getting Emotional Support

When you first open up about your story, it's natural to want to talk about it with others. There's a new freedom when you remove the shame you felt for so long. But I'll caution you to be careful who you share your story with. It's your story and you can choose how much of it and to whom you tell.

When I started therapy, my mother-in-law was kind enough to watch the baby while I went. She often asked me how therapy was going. Fresh from therapy, I would want to discuss many of the things that I had discovered and she listened. She seemed to be sympathetic until one day she verbally attacked me. I shared more than she could handle.

She told me that I was having a "pity party" and needed to stop. She was so angry and it was very hurtful. I had thought she was safe to talk to and liked the maternal acceptance I had felt. Then I believe she had heard enough, possibly felt triggered, and could no longer be supportive. I learned to limit the details of my story to a select few.

If you want to tell a loved one, let them know that you just need them to listen and give you support. They only need to believe you and let you know that they love you. Words like "I'm so sorry that happened to you" and "I don't know what to say except I love you" will help you to see that it's OK to be real about your story.

Not everyone can handle hearing about incest and child abuse. They may not know what to say and you can end up feeling even more isolated. Talking about child abuse is uncomfortable. Most people are just not equipped to be helpful and may respond in ways that are hurtful without intending to. Even your best friends may not respond well because they just don't know what to say. That's why it's so important to first share your story with a professional who's trained to lead you through the healing process.

PARENTING WELL AFTER CHILDHOOD ABUSE

There is a wonderful book, "You Can Help" by Rebecca Street, an incest survivor. It's a guide for loved ones of survivors offering practical advice on how to show understanding and support in the healing process.

I remember a particular writing exercise as one of the most helpful things I did in therapy. It was at a time when I got remarried and was struggling with being a step-parent and parenting my teenagers. I felt stuck and had some more healing to do.

My therapist asked me to write 3 letters (that I wouldn't send). The first one was to my father laying out all my feelings about what he had done to me. Then, I was to write what I imagined to be his response (denial, anger, refusal to accept responsibility). Finally, I wrote the letter that I would've liked to receive from my father (full of love and remorse).

Writing these letters was powerful. Sharing them with my therapist and having her help me explore and digest what I was feeling was very cathartic. I was able to let go of expecting anything that I wanted from my father. I hadn't realized how my longing for his validation was keeping me stuck.

By working with my therapist, I was able to get back on track and be there for my family.

I hope you now believe in the value of therapy and will seek it out to get to the root causes of your pain. It won't be easy but, with courage, you will finally be able to put the pain behind you.

Some therapists are better than others and it is a good idea to get a recommendation. It's important to take that first step. Just make an appointment and see how it goes. Honor your fear and resistance to telling a stranger your secrets, and

WHY GO TO THERAPY?

then move past it. They can help. If you don't connect with one therapist, get a different one.

You deserve to live a happy life. There is so much hope for the future of you and your children. Give yourself the love and respect that you didn't receive as a child. Therapy can lead the way.

Long before I started therapy I used writing as an outlet for my feelings. I find that getting my thoughts on paper and out of my head help to lessen their hold on me. I encourage you to try writing for yourself – don't worry it won't be graded.

The following page contains some practical ways to start connecting with your inner child. Use the writing exercise repeatedly until you believe that you weren't to blame.

Connect with Your Inner Child

Make sure you will not be interrupted for at least 30 minutes and have the tissues handy. You may need a sitter or have your kids in daycare to give yourself enough time. Caring for yourself is very important in order to take good care of anyone else.

Before doing any self-healing, start by relaxing. Sit or lie in bed and take deep breaths until you feel calm.

Can you remember what it felt like to be a child? What were some of your favorite things?

Ask yourself what you needed. What understanding and treatment did you deserve?

- Find photographs of your childhood. Look at pictures of yourself as a small child and try to find a connection. Notice what feelings and thoughts you have.

- Write a letter to your little child self – whatever age you picture when you think back to yourself at a tender time. Usually it is under age 8 that we are most impressionable and vulnerable. It's sad to say that after that age we can get hardened, put up the walls and your adult self may find it harder to feel tenderness toward the older child. Go back to when you were small and vulnerable. Soften your heart.

- Start writing or journaling. It's a valuable form of therapy for your wounded child. Often putting your thoughts on paper helps to clarify them and relieve their impact on you.

WHY GO TO THERAPY?

1. What would this child tell you? (Write it down, whatever first comes up)

2. What does this child need?

3. What would you like to say to this child?

4. Can you give this child love? Can you send acceptance and hugs to him/her?

5. Can you tell him or her that nothing was their fault, that they were doing a fine job of being a kid and it was the adults who messed up?

Chapter 3

Recognizing Denial

You may be in denial about being in denial. This chapter will help you to confront the ways that you may have downplayed your past. You'll have the added bonus of noticing other people using denial to mask their reality. You will learn the freedom that comes from looking at life realistically.

Children can normalize anything. When abused, children tend to take the blame for what happened and deny how bad it was. This cycle of denial needs to be addressed. I believe that my mother was abused as a child and in such denial that she let it happen to her own children. How I wish she had gotten help. It was a different time in the 1970s, when people didn't talk about abuse or mental health very much. Now there is no good excuse not to seek help.

How do you know that you're not OK? When you find yourself saying things that make the abuse sound palatable – or sticking up for your abuser – and your gut hurts.

When I was a young adult visiting my parents on a holiday, I would act like things were fine and then head directly to a bar or store to buy beer when I left. I was pretending that we were a good family when I really didn't feel any attachment to those people. The family secret was buried in denial and it made me feel gross to be around them. All our interactions were so fake.

When I wasn't with my family, I pretended that my childhood didn't have any impact on me. I thought I could live my life and put the past away. It wasn't that easy. By hiding my painful past under layers of jokes and partying I was letting it fester and it came out in uncontrollable ways.

My denial didn't help me to see the reasons for my anger and distrust. I found myself jealous of boyfriends and ever ready to pounce on any dishonesty as if it were the last straw. I felt that I had to be vigilant to make sure no one hurt me. I never fully trusted anyone. I had angry outbursts and unproductive fights with my boyfriends.

I felt triggered and scared whenever I felt that someone was trying to control me. I felt incapable of having a healthy relationship and blamed it on the men I was picking. Therapy was the way I finally accepted that I had to deal with my past to have any hope for the future.

Why do you stay in denial?

It's understandable why you want to remember the happy family and pretend the ugliness didn't exist. Denial is easy to maintain because your memories aren't all bad. You want to keep the good and minimize the bad. Once you see things clearly it can be the other way around for a while. One day you can achieve some balance when thinking about your childhood.

I have some great family memories from when my older sisters were home and there were 6 of us in the family. We would have family game nights and there was such laughter. It was magical when my sisters would joke around and start laughing so hard they couldn't stop. Even my mom would be laughing along. I loved times around the dinner table when

RECOGNIZING DENIAL

everyone would be happy. I idolized my older sisters, they were so pretty, smart and funny.

In our family there was 8 years in between two sets of daughters. My oldest pair were one year apart then 8 years later, Terri and I were born 18 months apart. This made it feel like two different families for me. Once there was 6 of us and then 4.

Everything changed shortly after my second oldest sister left for college. My mother had been fighting with her and must've felt relief mixed with sadness when she left. She felt an empty nest but still had two little girls at home. I was 8 and Terri was almost 10. That's when my father's attention turned to us and it felt like my mother abandoned caring for us.

Mother decided to go to work and apparently didn't want to be a wife and mother anymore. She was very unhappy at home. She wasn't in touch with her feelings, although she expressed anger and resentment easily. She showed us how to get stuck in unhappiness and live there. Denial was her mode of operation and it made her miserable.

Denial is a coping mechanism that can eat away at your soul, but you may have been taught that keeping the secret was the only option. When you were abused as a child you couldn't rationalize what was happening and were susceptible to others in your family suppressing the reality. You may have been told outright not to talk about it or you saw that it was an unacceptable subject by others' denial. "Tell Grandma you fell off the swing."

When I tried to confide to my mother about a couple of significant secrets in my young life, she betrayed my trust and told my father. This taught me that she wasn't to be trusted and couldn't help me, especially against my father. She didn't like to discuss unpleasant subjects. She taught us well not to talk about uncomfortable things. She couldn't say the word "brassiere" without whispering.

My best friend, Bonnie, lived down the street and her family was completely open. Going there was such a breath of fresh air. Her parents were playful with each other, affectionate and would talk about everything. There were Playboy magazines in their bathroom, but it didn't seem perverted. It was out in the open and normalized that way. Her mom would talk and laugh with us about boys. We got good advice from her. I was always astounded at the things Bonnie could tell her mom.

Bonnie's house was a happy place to go and I spent as much time there as possible. They had company and friends over often. My parents never had people at our house.

Being around their family really saved me. It gave me a picture of honesty and how to deal with the ups and downs of life. They argued, debated and made up. Bonnie could speak her mind to her parents. It was amazing how differently our families operated.

Secrecy and denial were the order of the day in our house. Pretense and lies. It was enough to make you feel crazy. Denial was normal but I began to see that it wasn't healthy.

Terri and I would talk about our parents being hypocrites and how much we hated them. We called our father a sick pervert. It was disgusting to see him interact with waitresses or any women. We couldn't see him any other way than a creep. We didn't deny the truth but had to hide it. We didn't tell any adults, only our closest friends.

After we left home my sister and I would often talk about our parents. She started therapy when she moved to Tennessee for college, long before I did. She always encouraged me to get counseling. I benefited from what she shared from her therapists.

Terri maintained that our mother must have known about the abuse and I would adamantly defend her innocence. I really wanted to deny the possibility that she could've known and not done anything. It was unfathomable to me because I knew that she loved us.

Some years later my mother was asking me why Terri wouldn't talk to them. It was a rare moment of honesty and I felt that I was going to give her a news flash. I told her that Terri didn't want to see our father again because he had molested us. She seemed sad when she said, "Oh, I thought something like that was going on." I was blown away.

She dropped a bomb on my denial. She knew? How could she suspect her husband was hurting her daughters and want to believe it wasn't true so badly that she could blindly look the other way? That is the definition of denial.

She had a separate bedroom from my father's that was in the same hallway as our bedrooms. Of course, she knew. How I wish she had slept with the door open and protected us from his break ins. I'm sure she heard his slippers shuffle and slide down the hallway like we did.

I was taught the art of denial by the master. My mother knew but didn't let herself think about it. There were incongruencies in what I felt was happening and how everyone in the family acted.

We were a good, happy family to the neighbors and at church; but at home my parents barely spoke to each other and my sister and I tried to stay away from them. We lived for the day we would be able to leave and would magically become happy with that freedom.

However, living under the control of a tyrant and his miserable wife affected us in ways that were hard to shake off once we were free. The denial stuck with me for a long time. I kept wanting to be the peacekeeper in the family.

D.E.N.I.A.L. stands for: Don't Even Notice I Am Lying

Does this sound familiar? You want others to believe what you're portraying and not find out what's hidden underneath. It's understandable why you would do this but it's not healthy.

The subject of sexual child abuse is horrible and unthinkable. Our brains naturally want to reject the thought immediately. It's happening at an alarming rate. The statistics are unfathomable.

1 in 4 girls will experience sexual assault before they are 18 and it's 1 in 6 for boys. Google it if you don't believe me.

We must face the truth and talk about the problem to shine light on it. Secrets perpetuate in the dark. Denying it doesn't make it go away.

Shame and embarrassment may be why you don't want to admit that you were abused. This is a vicious cycle. Your inner pain needs to be reversed to the rightful owner – your abuser. They're the only one who should bear the burden but often seem to get off scot-free.

Over the years, many friends have come out and told me that they were sexually abused. There's always a sadness conveyed and a kind of acceptance when they told me, "You know, it happened to me too."

So many men and women are carrying this pain and shame around with them. It just isn't a subject that comes up in conversation very often. I'm changing that in my life. It

RECOGNIZING DENIAL

doesn't feel good, it's uncomfortable, but not talking about it feels that way too. Denying the effects of abuse is painful.

If you continue to deny that the abuse was hurtful, you run the risk of letting it continue around you. Of course, you won't abuse your children but someone else may. You may be blinded to the signs or outright deny it if you are told.

"It wasn't that bad", "It happened a long time ago", "I'm OK now". These are things that I said and thought whenever I allowed myself to remember my childhood abuse. I was in the long-standing habit of minimizing what happened to me in the past.

As an adult, I rationalized that things could have been worse, and I wasn't under the control of anyone who could hurt me.

This was adult thinking and there was a wounded child inside that needed me to address what happened. I had been neglecting the small voice inside that was screaming for attention.

If you're in denial you are probably downplaying your inner child's voice. How does this voice try to get your attention?

You have the innate belief that something is wrong with you.

You think you don't deserve anything good.

You believe you can't get respect or love from anyone.

You engage in self-destructive behaviors like drinking, drugs and sex to feel better and numb yourself.

You feel emotionally unstable, having sudden outbursts of anger at seemingly little things.

You feel triggered by hearing about child abuse.

PARENTING WELL AFTER CHILDHOOD ABUSE

You experience fear, anger, self-loathing, hopelessness, or intense sadness that seem to come out of nowhere.

These are all symptoms of deep-seated pain that hasn't been properly addressed.

P.A.I.N. stands for: Pay Attention Inward Now

You feel bad but pretend that you don't. This is a ticking time bomb. If you continue to deny something as painful as abuse when you were at your most vulnerable, the pain will keep trying to resurface. This could lead to health issues and self-destructive behaviors.

When you can't lash out at the perpetrator, due to your denial of who is to blame, your choice is to hurt yourself. You may feel so badly about yourself that you pick abusive partners, put yourself in dangerous situations and abuse your body with drugs or alcohol.

When you realize that your pain is running your life you must get help.

Another symptom of denial is to believe the abuse to be mostly your fault. Because of this, I didn't think about it happening to others in the family. I felt that it was contained between my father and his daughters. My older sisters didn't think about telling anyone and protecting the sisters who were left at home when they went off to college. Their denial let them think it wouldn't happen to us. I never blamed them for this because they weren't equipped to protect us.

I was also in denial about the physical and emotional abuse that I suffered. I didn't believe that I was physically abused as a child until I told a counselor some stories. She told me that "Being dragged by your hair, thrown to the floor and kicked, and slapped across the face are all instances of physical abuse." Oh yeah, I guess so. I was more traumatized by the sneaking into my bedroom at night. I thought I was only affected by the sexual abuse.

It took years of my sister telling me that all the fault rested on our dad, and then some good counseling sessions, to break through my denial. When she would talk to me, I thought "that's fine for you to believe, but I still feel like it was my fault."

When you're forced to live a lie, it's not normal for you to think of yourself in a good way. Lying feels naughty. You end up feeling rotten and find it hard to be kind to yourself. You may find it hard to be truthful. You don't know how to express what you need in relationships. When you get released from the prison of abuse it's not automatic to be able to live normally. Therapy is needed to rehabilitate your thinking. At least this was my experience.

You're worth working on yourself. Be brave enough to break out of the habit of denial and enter the realm of the truth. It really will set you free.

The book "The Courage to Heal" is an oldy but goody, published in 1988. It is a guide for women survivors of child sexual abuse. I had to order it from Kmart (before internet shopping was a thing) and was nervous picking it up at the store. But this action was a big step in my own "courage to heal". I found the book invaluable and I highly recommend it. This was the first book that spoke to my issues with clarity and understanding.

How I Got Out of Denial

Number one, I had to trust my feelings and forgive myself for coping however I needed to in the past. I learned to be kinder to myself.

I had to find, and then listen to, my authentic voice. I needed to know who I was instead of the person I often pretended to be.

I practiced not trying to please everyone or care about what they thought. I had to see my feelings as important and learn not to stuff them away.

I caught myself when I slipped back into feeling like it wasn't so bad and I had no right to complain. I had to tune into the present, how I was feeling and realize that I was lying to myself.

I had to be my own cheerleader to keep resisting old behaviors. I practiced saying positive words about myself instead of negative ones.

I also relied on my sister to help me remember it wasn't my fault and how lovable I was. Terrin* made me remember we were innocent children. Truly, if I didn't have her support, I may have buried the whole thing.

Terrin gave me such love and acceptance. We would frequently call each other and cry after either of us had a therapy session.

*(Terri changed her name to Terrin as an adult and will be referred to correctly hereafter in this book.)

When you stop denying reality you may face some struggles. The other family members who are used to you propping up their own denial won't like it. They'll tell you something is wrong with you. Why would you want to bring up bad things from the past?

They have their own reasons for hiding behind imaginary memories. They may not be allies in your healing. You can only lead by example. You must find other people who will support you.

RECOGNIZING DENIAL

Once you remove the veil of secrecy and allow yourself to accept the reality of what happened, it will get better. It's a relief to stop lying to yourself and others. Give yourself the gift of calling yourself a survivor. You may have been a victim when you were young – but you had an inner strength that helped you survive.

Give yourself credit for all that you have overcome and believe that you can handle whatever comes next.

I hope you better understand the use of denial and are ready to live honestly. You can see that denial is incongruent to living your truth. You don't want to pass down this hypocrisy to your children. It will be necessary to set boundaries with anyone who wants to keep you in denial. The next chapter will show you the importance of healthy boundaries.

Chapter 4
Setting Boundaries

Boundaries are what's OK and what's not OK for you. It's a personal choice to draw a line and let others know that there is a line. This is a healthy way to keep others from taking advantage of or hurting you.

When you were young you may not have been taught about boundaries. I know I wasn't. I heard about it as an adult and thought, "What? You mean I can determine what I will and won't tolerate from other people?"

It was a foreign concept to me because my feelings and needs were overrun as a child. My body was not my own, I had no voice to say "No" to my parents. I was taken advantage of and didn't have any rights.

When I got to be a preteen and more headstrong, I rebelled and said "No" to my dad. I locked my door and learned that he couldn't open it when I wedged a tennis shoe under it. Locked bedroom doors never stopped him. He didn't see it as a boundary – he just unlocked it and came in.

How sick is that? When a child locks you out and you think it's a game to win. He won all right – he won hatred and fear, resentment and unhappy children. He got to be the first man to break his daughters' hearts.

If my mother would have known anything about boundaries, she could've told him that it was not OK for him to break into our rooms at night. She could have told him to stop. All I wanted was for someone to make him stop. She could've said we needed to tell her if he touched us again. If she were stronger, she may have taken our side instead of his.

I felt like she gave up on us and "threw us to the wolf". Shutting my heart down to the people who I once loved and depended on was hurtful. I hardened my heart at home – for a decade.

It hasn't been a good strategy for dealing with conflict in my adult life. I struggle with figuring out what I need and being direct about it. I often have trouble using my voice. I feel that I communicate well in the positive, but I struggle with any conflict.

I learned the necessity of setting boundaries for my kids though. I wanted them to know about respecting boundaries and that they could set them with anyone they chose. There will be much more about this in the Child Safety chapter in Part 2.

How do you teach kids about boundaries? When they are having conflict, you teach them to stand up for themselves and say "No, I don't like that." They have the power of words to defend themselves. By treating children with respect, they will learn their value and have confidence to voice their opinions with their peers.

We want them to speak up when someone is taking advantage of them or asking them to do anything they don't want to do. If they have a strange feeling about a person or situation, they need to trust their gut and get away from it.

This is taught by seeing their parents be assertive. It doesn't mean that you go around looking for conflict, but when something happens that crosses a line, you can take the opportunity to use your voice. You don't want to let anyone

SETTING BOUNDARIES

who crosses a boundary get away with it. Model how adults handle conflicts.

If a neighbor's big dog keeps getting loose, you can say to yourself, "Oh well. People suck. There's nothing I can do about it." But this is victim behavior. When you see yourself as a capable adult you can go to them and say "I'm concerned about your dog getting loose. It's a safety issue for your dog and the neighborhood kids. What steps can you take to fix the problem?"

Even if you think that another person has done something rude and malicious, you can give the benefit of the doubt and try to resolve it without them getting defensive. Children will learn a lot from watching you be fair with people. Often you get respect by being respectful.

When your kids become adults don't get mad when they practice setting boundaries with you. It's a good thing. One of my friends excitedly told me she planned to spend a whole month with her daughter when her new grandbaby was born. But when the time came, her daughter told her that they weren't taking guests until a week had passed so that they could bond with the baby. Then she told her mom she could only visit for one week at a time. I knew that this must have stung my friend's heart, but it was what her daughter had decided. It was appropriate for the new mom to set the boundaries clearly.

This is where honest communication comes into play. When you establish that even tough subjects are acceptable, you can discuss your differing expectations.

Along with accepting other's setting boundaries with you, you must become aware of who you haven't set healthy boundaries with.

If you still hold self-blame, you could be lax about abuse happening to your children. You may not believe it could happen to other children around your abuser. You may still let abusive family members babysit for you. If they didn't take good care of you, there's no reason to trust that they will treat your children better.

You can set boundaries of how much your children are around your original family. It's your duty to protect them from harm.

Take baby steps or giant leaps when you're thinking of setting new boundaries with your family of origin. Just because you have always gone to the family gathering on a holiday doesn't mean that you can't change that if you choose. You can do whatever you want now that you're an adult.

It may be the best thing for your children to be spared going where there is tension or drama. You're not obligated to take care of people's feelings who didn't take care of yours. Give yourself permission to make your own choices about what you want in your life. What's the worst that can happen?

Start by surrounding yourself with good, positive people. Are there toxic people in your life? Is there any reason that you must be close to them? Set boundaries to give them less of your time and energy or remove them from your life completely. Eventually, if you no longer play their games of drama or negativity, they will move on. It takes two to tangle.

It's a gift to yourself to get away from negativity. You deserve to be loved for who you are, and it starts with accepting yourself.

Learning to set boundaries is a valuable quest for those of us who had our lines crossed at an early age. Respecting other

SETTING BOUNDARIES

people's boundaries is also a good lesson for us. Sometimes we want to control everything so much that we step on other people's wishes.

It's understandable why abused children want to feel in control when they grow up. It can be a barrier to relationships though. No one wants to be controlled by another. It's necessary to share in decisions and allow another's choices to be just as acceptable as yours are. Overcoming the need to control situations can help you to relax a bit. You don't have to be in charge of everything.

Practice setting boundaries until you become good at it. Don't do what you don't want to do. You aren't obligated to make everyone else happy. It seems so simple, but many people have a really hard time setting boundaries and then are miserable or stressed with all their commitments.

Just say "No, sorry, I'm not available". This could empower someone else to take over and get things done. You're great – but not the only super-human around.

Teaching our kids to speak up and set boundaries for what they find acceptable is a GIFT. It is a choice we wish that we had had.

So far, we've discussed breaking the cycle, getting out of denial and setting boundaries. Each of these subjects can take repetition and reminders to become habits. Next, we'll explore the need for learning to be kind to yourself to be a healthy parent.

Chapter 5

Learning to Be Kind to Yourself

> "If you want someone to be happy – practice compassion.
> If you want to be happy – practice compassion."
>
> —Dalai Lama

For me, the key to shedding the past was learning how to be kind to myself. I had to change behaviors that I wasn't proud of. Smoking, drinking too much, losing jobs and being promiscuous reinforced my negative thoughts about myself. Little by little I got out of debt, stopped drinking to oblivion and limited my friends to ones that were good for me. It took some time, but I finally made better dating choices too.

I learned that happiness could be achieved by striving to do what made me feel good about myself.

The goal isn't trying to be perfect – just better, healthier. If there's something that you feel ashamed about, it's definitely worth stopping. Step by step, you can lose the shame and point your life in a new direction by making choices in line with healing and taking care of yourself.

What do you need to do to live without regrets?

Accept Yourself

Survivors of child abuse can have low self-esteem, negative thoughts about themselves and feel unworthy of love. It's imperative that you stop this vicious cycle of thinking. These thoughts were put in your head by abusive parents and you must break free and see yourself in a new light.

Be gentle and accepting of your faults instead of thinking that they reinforce your unworthiness. Change how you talk to yourself. See that you have many good qualities. Focus on the positives and try not to dwell on the negatives.

List your accomplishments. Go ahead take a minute and write down anything you have done that you feel good about. It can be graduating high school, being respected at work, paying your bills, getting yourself out of a depressed state, being a good friend, etc.

Now, this one may be harder. Look at yourself as you are today and list attributes that you like about yourself. They can be physical, you have a nice smile; or deeper, you are trustworthy. If you find yourself pausing and having trouble, give yourself a break. Think about what your best friend (or dog) would list as your good qualities. Oh, if we could only be the people our dogs think we are!

Show yourself kindness daily. If you are having a rough day, look in the mirror and tell yourself "I'm OK. I am trying my best. Tomorrow will be better." It's true, things do look better in the morning. Some days your thinking can be so destructive and negative that you feel hopeless. Distract yourself with something else until you can sleep on it.

Surround yourself with positive words and signs. Be your own cheerleader. Find your inner strength to support yourself. Lifting yourself up is no one else's job, no matter how much they love you.

LEARNING TO BE KIND TO YOURSELF

Find affirmations that work for you – put up sticky notes on your mirror. It may seem silly but having positive messages around to combat the negative will help. "You look marvelous." "You are loved." "You matter."

I recommend Rebecca Street's YouCanHelpSurvivors.com website where you can sign up for the "Six weeks of healing conversation for survivors of sexual abuse and assault". You will get a short daily email that is very helpful for motivation and practical tips. Even though I feel that I have done 80% of my healing – I still found these reminders invaluable.

Her "conversations" help you to see that you are not alone. Many survivors experience the same feelings that you do. It comforted me to know that these shared feelings of distrust and depression could be overcome.

Many survivors feel badly about themselves without understanding where it comes from. Notice your self-talk. Can you show yourself the kindness that you wish you had gotten as a child? When you make mistakes, allow yourself to see it as normal. Being human is not proof that you are unworthy.

Do you have a feeling of something holding you back from freedom and happiness? Do you feel your neck and shoulders tense most of the time? There was a monkey put on your back in your formative years, but you can shake it off. Imagine that heaviness as a coat – and take it off.

My last therapist explained to me that when I was holding onto the pain of my father's actions, it was like trying to fly with him holding onto my foot. If I could kick him free, then I would be lighter and able to soar away. Envisioning that made sense to me.

Practice self-care. Take a bath, get a massage, give yourself flowers. Write yourself a love letter, or at least an encouraging sticky note.

Breathe and free your mind. Say "I deserve to be happy. I am an adult. I'm the master of my state of mind. It's no one else's job to give me what I need. I'm the best person for the job."

I needed to look in the mirror and remind myself that I was a capable, adult woman. I felt like such a wounded child at times. Especially on days that I discussed something painful in therapy.

Practice – Practice – Practice. It may feel like you're taking baby steps – which is fine. You may slip into old ways of thinking. That's OK too. The difference is that you will notice when you feel that pain of self-hate and you'll get better at turning it around. It's a worthwhile endeavor to bring your self-image from garbage to worthy.

Healthy and Happy Parents Take Care of Themselves

Remember when you're on a plane and the instructions are to "Put on your own oxygen mask before you assist anyone else"? Of course, that's because you can't help another if you're running out of breath yourself.

Every parent needs a break from the day in and day out of taking care of others. You must find ways to recharge. Don't feel guilty about doing things for yourself – because it is ultimately good for your family.

What? You don't have time to think about yourself? You can't afford to get a babysitter and take an exercise class? These things may be partially true – but if you are working

LEARNING TO BE KIND TO YOURSELF

on taking care of your needs, I bet there's something you can work out.

Consider what you can do in the following categories that don't have to cost a lot.

1. Health: you can take walks, get a yoga DVD, go to a produce market and get fresh fruits and veggies.

2. Interests: reading, gardening, art, church, hobbies...

3. Date Night: Couples need to get connected away from the kids. A strong partnership will enhance the security at home.

A counselor gave me the good advice that while on date night: Don't talk about the kids. It's tempting, but find other things to discuss to help you remember that you are more than a mom or dad. Do something that you used to love as a childless couple. If you don't have a partner – make a date with a friend.

4. Play: Play can be remarkably healing. While you are parenting your own child, you can reparent yourself. Give yourself permission to be silly, laugh, roll on the ground and play with your kids. Get yourself out of your adult world and into theirs.

Make silly faces, have a contest for who has the silliest. Play dress-up. Let your kids be the guides. Being an authentic person means letting your guard down and allowing yourself to be free of judgement. Your kids don't care if you can sing well, just that you are gleefully singing and dancing around the room with them.

Times like these make up a happy childhood. I would often think to myself "I am having my happy childhood now." Be present in the moment and enjoy it. You can get back to work or chores when the time comes.

Happy Mom/Dad = Happy family. By learning to take care of yourself you are modeling healthy behavior for your children.

Practice Being Present

> "The Past is gone,
> The Future is not here yet,
> Now, I am free of both"
>
> – Deepak Chopra

I'm a massage therapist. While I am working, I have time to think. I will start out focusing on the client and what I feel going on in their body, but often my mind will drift off and my hands just follow the routine that I've done a thousand times already. The calming music and dim lights are conducive to letting my mind figure out grocery lists or my life's purpose. Often my mind is going over conversations and situations where I should have done or said something better. Why am I so bad at thinking on the spot of something witty to say?

Recently, I was thinking about being present and how it's not an automatic thing for me. I know it's a struggle for most people in this fast-paced age. But I was this way as a child, and I think it hurt my ability to focus as an adult. I recall always looking forward to the future, just getting through whatever was in front of me to get to something better.

My mind set up blocks to shield me from my reality – living with an unstable mother and a dangerous father. After years of having my brain stay a little bit removed while my life was going on, it was trained to do that on a regular basis.

LEARNING TO BE KIND TO YOURSELF

I also lived for the future when my kids were small, and I was home alone with them. Every day was full of challenges and I just kept them busy; going somewhere outside, playing on the floor, plopping them in front of the TV. I don't think I was always enjoying every little moment like I wish I had.

I remember feeling like – just get through it until naptime. Then, two more hours until bedtime. This makes me feel like I was being selfish. But I realize that I was doing the best I could at the time.

My emotional state was a wreck then, I was going through therapy and then a divorce. I was there with my children, laughing and interacting, but I felt like there was a barrier/glass wall keeping me from enjoying the moments and being truly present.

Looking to the future when things would be easier was a necessary way to cope while growing up. Even though I don't need to any more, it seems to be my subconscious switch-over. We all need reminding to be present.

My sister, Terrin's wise words: "Be Here Now" about the present, and "Be There Then" about the future, often reverberate in my mind.

Finally, I am aware of my tendency not to be present and must constantly work on it in my beautiful life. I must make a conscious effort to notice what's going on around me, really listen to what people are saying and breathe in the space that I'm in. The future is only an idea – all we truly have is the present.

Hopefully you realize the importance of becoming the best person you can be for your kids. Working on self-love and being present will help achieve this goal.

If you're hard on yourself, you're harder on others too. Being kinder and more accepting of yourself will help you to be that for your children. Your kids need you to step up and work on loving yourself so that you can model being a healthy person.

You will also need to love and respect yourself to have a healthy, adult relationship. The next chapter will explore some of the struggles that abuse survivors often face in relationships.

Chapter 6

Relationships and Divorce

Good Relationships with Your Kids

Most of this chapter is about adult relationships but I want to touch on making sure that you develop loving, closeness with your kids.

Since I didn't have good relationships with either of my parents, I needed to figure out how to foster it with my own kids. Of course, I loved them but making sure that they knew it and that I showed it often was important to me.

I remember a friend telling me that she loved her 9 year-old daughter but didn't like her some of the time. It shook me because I knew that they were close. I believe I was taken aback because I felt that was what my mother did to me. It seemed that she decided she didn't like me. I understood later that my friend was just venting about her daughter's behavior.

Later, when my daughter was around age 10, I realized that we weren't as close as I wanted us to be. Sierra was the easy one, rarely disobeyed me or caused any trouble. It was as if she was flying under my radar and I wasn't giving her enough attention. Her brother, Devin, was louder, mischievous and seemed to take more of my time.

I had to realize what I had needed at age 10 and give it to my daughter.

I wanted to make sure that I listened to my daughter and encouraged her to use her voice to get what she wanted. She was used to going with the flow because her nature was so easy going. However, I gave her a turn to decide which movie or restaurant we would all go to. I didn't want her to get in the habit of thinking "It doesn't matter, whatever someone else wants is fine." There are times when we all need to know what we want and be able to ask for it directly.

I vowed to make more effort to connect with her and it worked. She flourished under my compliments and involvement in her interests. I am so glad that I gave her more of myself because when she became a pre-teen I may have lost the opportunity.

Maybe part of the reason our relationship was behind was subconscious. At age 10, I felt that my mother pulled away from me and didn't give me positive attention. Perhaps I was about to repeat the pattern. Because I was working on parenting better, I made a conscious decision to remedy the situation.

It didn't take much for me to develop more closeness with Sierra, I just had to realize that it was lacking and make up for it.

Pay attention to the child that may not be demanding it. Be sure to give individual time to each of your kids when you can. Develop the closeness, trust and affection that may have been absent in your childhood.

Adult Relationships

Many survivors struggle with adult relationships. Being abused makes it harder to trust others, accept love, use your voice and experience true intimacy. This knowledge is based

RELATIONSHIPS AND DIVORCE

on my own experiences, things I learned in couples' counseling and many books on the subject. I don't claim to be an expert, but I have been in many relationships and am in my second marriage. I have done a lot of work on myself to be able to be in a healthy relationship.

Relationships are hard, marriage is work. These are things you hear but may not fully understand until you have been in a committed relationship for a few years. At first, it's magical to be in love. You walk on air and can't stop thinking about how wonderful the other person is. They make you feel so wonderful and special too. You both seem to vibrate with this energy of love.

You see all the good qualities you've been searching for in your new love. It seems like your fairy tale is coming true. You show your own best qualities and are the great, loving person that your partner thinks you are. Naturally you don't want to fall from grace and show any negative parts of yourself. As a survivor you may not trust this person with all of your story. You may be afraid to share your childhood experiences because you fear rejection.

You may act confident around a new person but feel differently inside. This creates a falseness that you know will break down one day. This is why people are shocked when their lover turns into a completely different person down the line. It could take months or years.

Is this a real relationship if you don't show your true self, warts and all? Eventually you need to be honest. It's especially important to share all of yourself with a partner so they can be prepared to understand and help in your healing.

There is no "happily ever after" without some disagreements, problems and struggles. Trust and good communication are essential to getting through life with someone else. How do you learn to trust who you have chosen? How do you learn to communicate well if you have low self-esteem and don't feel like an equal partner?

Sometimes it's easier to argue about the small things because there's an underlying bigger issue that you aren't able to address. You may yell about the socks on the floor when you're actually feeling disrespected and treated like a housekeeper. I think this is true for most couples but it's especially challenging when you are an abuse survivor.

You may have trouble using your voice and being assertive to get what you need. You may not feel worthy of speaking up or aren't tuned in to what's really bothering you. You may want to avoid conflict at all costs, but the cost could be your soul.

If you don't learn to speak up, give your opinions or set boundaries; you risk losing yourself to someone else's wishes. It may feel like you are out of control and susceptible to emotional abuse from your partner. You must find a balance of being true to yourself while allowing the other person to be themselves.

It's important to not identify a partner with your abuser, even when they remind you of them.

Speaking your mind doesn't have to mean war. If you learn to talk about how you're feeling, then things can get resolved or understood. It's OK to disagree with your partner and say so. You need to realize that you won't be struck down like you were as a child.

You can't keep feelings bottled up inside without repercussions. Festering resentment will lead to an eventual blowup or health issue. Unresolved conflicts can make you run away from the relationship feeling hopeless to change anything.

RELATIONSHIPS AND DIVORCE

If the relationship is worth it and, especially when there are kids involved, you owe it to everyone to stick it out and work on the issues.

Survivors must learn to tune into themselves to figure out how they feel and what they need. Often you may be triggered by something and not understand why you are so upset. It takes practice to stay present when you learned to shut down your feelings as a child.

You must learn to assert your opinions and share your feelings. Do you have a partner you feel safe doing this with? Hopefully, you aren't in a relationship with someone who reminds you of one of your parents or your abuser.

Often, a person who felt unloved by their parents will seek out similar people as adults to try to fix the past. If you had an alcoholic father, you may gravitate towards a drinker and try to make them love you as you had hoped your dad would. Don't get caught up in trying to "fix" people. Ideally, relationships are there to help us grow and get to our best selves.

You learned from an early age about the roles of husband and wife from watching your parents. Whether good or bad, their interactions shaped your views on what is "normal". Fighting and crying can become familiar to you. Maybe one person had control and the other quietly submitted and showed resentment.

That's how I saw my parents. They had a miserable marriage. I learned that the male had the power and females were dependent and inferior. My mother was shutdown, aloof and mean to her kids. She was angry with her husband but took it out on her children. We were all afraid of my father's power.

You can decide that you'll never have a relationship like the one your parents had. It will take a lot of healing and work to learn new, healthy patterns. I'm still working on being assertive with my voice and not shutting down.

It's hard to break out of patterns that you learned when you were small. You must work to have a better partnership for the benefit of your kids. It's important for you to show your kids a good, working relationship.

There can be arguments followed by apologies. There can be heated discussions that don't get out of hand. It's good for kids to see that people who love each other can work things out.

Conflict

In relationship conflicts, it's helpful if you can focus on what your goal outcome is rather than trying to prove yourself the one who is right. Most couples find themselves arguing their own position, digging their heels in to be right and make the other person finally agree. This won't allow either person to fully hear the other's point. It's much more productive and loving to go into discussions trying to bring back harmony.

I like to use the word "request" when stating something I need from my husband. It's received much better than a demand and he has something concrete to work on. Try saying, "I have a request...can you do that?"

Requesting help is a good tactic to use with children too. Requests signal respect, you are not demanding or whining, just asking for what you need.

Another valuable trick for staying connected, is to hold hands when you are discussing a problem. It softens your tone and keeps each person calm. It's not always easy to do but can keep things from escalating. Try it – with your partner and your kids.

Second marriages are where you get to use what you learned from past mistakes and work harder on the relationship. Early on with my second husband, I requested that we agree to let the person who feels most strongly about a subject get to be the decider about it.

For example: I had an issue when my husband would startle me while I was getting dressed. Because I experienced my father being a "Peeping Tom" when I was a teenager, I have anxiety and value my privacy immensely.

I always close the bathroom door when I'm in the shower, but don't lock it. However, I would get upset when my husband would walk in the bathroom when I was undressed. It wasn't a rational feeling, but a gut reaction when I wasn't expecting him.

I finally asked him to announce himself or knock before entering so that I wouldn't get triggered. He didn't understand and tried to brush it off saying, "What? I'm not allowed to see you naked?"

I found my voice, because it was important to me, and told him why I felt so threatened when he would startle me. I said I knew that he didn't mean to sneak up on me, but I felt strongly that I needed to feel safe in my home. I didn't want to have to lock the door.

He was understanding and realized that it was a little thing for him to knock when it was so important to me.

It's important to discern where the strongest feelings lie and this just takes investigating the question, "Who feels more strongly about this issue?"

PARENTING WELL AFTER CHILDHOOD ABUSE

Even when you make requests, focus on the goal, assert your voice and determine who is the decider on an issue there will still be disagreements. When you live with someone you'll have to find ways to settle your differences.

Most people don't really know how to argue effectively. Like kids, adults just want to be heard and understood. Sometimes couples don't learn to listen to each other until they go to counseling. Learning the technique of active listening is truly game changing.

Active listening is when one person gets to talk while the other listens without interrupting. When the point is made, the listener repeats back what they heard by saying "What I heard you say is ..." Then the speaker can clarify what they said and meant.

An example of clarifying, "No, honey. I didn't say that I hate your mother and never want her to visit. I merely asked how long she would be staying."

In this instance the listener believes that their partner doesn't like their mother and heard that they didn't want her to visit. But that wasn't what was said.

Can you see how your thinking can make another's innocent statement sound exactly how you thought it would? If you are willing to take some responsibility for the miscommunication, you can work on trying to be open and curious.

Believing the thoughts that are engraved in our minds isn't easy to change. The system of questioning your thoughts by Byron Katie really helped me to start. It's called "The Work" and is a path to sanity. Truly. My kids told me that they could tell it was helping me after I went to a workshop of hers. I have many of her books and CDs.

RELATIONSHIPS AND DIVORCE

When I'm stuck in my negative thinking, I can write down my belief and then challenge my thoughts to find out if it's true. Often, I find out that my own thinking is getting in the way. For example, if I didn't believe the thought that my husband doesn't respect my opinion – I would be able to voice it more easily. I would just say what I need to say.

There are all kinds of stresses that life will throw at you. Jobs, money, exes, family, and those darling kids you decided to have; can make you feel frustrated enough to take it out on one another. It would be grand if couples could bond against stress and handle it together. More likely it will cause them to fight. It's good to remember that you are on the same team and try to find solutions together.

Couples' Counseling can really make a difference if you are both willing to take some responsibility for the problems and have a desire to make it work.

Marriage is a partnership, and each person can take care of different things for the good of the whole. Each person is not going to be exactly in tune with the other or have the same skills. You don't want to be married to yourself. That's why opposites attract.

Self-love is the most important and lasting relationship. Perhaps you need to change something about yourself and not your partner. Have confidence that you deserve love. Treat yourself well and don't allow disrespect.

It's been hard for me to figure out my triggers, why I'm feeling stressed and asserting my needs in a relationship. My opinions were suppressed when I was young and my father was the one in control.

I know that I learned to keep my mouth shut, hold in my feelings of anger and seethe with hatred towards my parents – for years. This was a coping mechanism that got me through my teenage years. However, I've noticed that I shut down in conflicts in my adult relationships and it doesn't serve me well at all.

When I feel that my husband isn't listening to me when I do speak up, the old familiar feelings of seething anger set in. When he doesn't agree with my opinion and brushes it off, I shut down. We had many conflicts over our different parenting tactics.

At times it's felt like I was under my father's control again with no rights or respect.

I've felt hopeless and considered divorce rather than confront my husband with my feelings. Because of my trust issues, it seems I often have "one foot out the door." I realize that I have every right to ask to be treated like an equal partner in our marriage, but it's not easy.

Marriage counseling helped us both to get on the same team. I realized how insecure I was feeling and that I needed to speak up with my views, even if I believed my husband wouldn't agree.

Our counselor said "You need to be more assertive. Your husband is a nice guy, you've been together a long time and he's safe to practice this with." I had to think about this because I really didn't feel like he was safe to argue with. I realized that his anger wouldn't hurt me, but thinking and feeling are very different things for me.

Teamwork. Families are like a sports team.

Parenting can bring out big differences in thinking between two parents. There are always compromises and disagreements between adults who are parenting – whether you are biological, step, adoptive, same sex, grands or exes.

With honest communication, your different expectations can be discussed.

Ideally you are all pulling for each other and don't have unhealthy competition for who is right and who's doing it best. You encourage and commiserate when needed. The parents are the coach and assistant coach, you can take turns on this depending on who is the expert in each situation. The kids are what hold the team together. They're the reason you are all on the field.

Families pull together and encourage each other when they're doing well and during times they need to try harder. Remind your partner that you are on the same team. Remember to tag team when one of you is getting too beat up.

Sometimes people are better off parenting separately.

Divorce

Unfortunately, many people find that they can't stay with their children's other parent and end up parenting alone. This is very sad for everyone. You must first choose wisely who you're having sex with. If you can't see this person as a good parent – use four condoms and a backup method.

When you're a single parent you'll have to find people who can help you. Whether it's with carpooling or having playdates. Get a team together. Everyone needs and appreciates help, so work together for the good of the kids.

"It takes a village." Raising kids doesn't have to be done alone. Of course, you need to find others who are trustworthy. Hopefully you can work it out to co-parent with your ex.

PARENTING WELL AFTER CHILDHOOD ABUSE

While I had chosen a really calm, sweet guy to marry and have kids with, unfortunately, we didn't end up living happily ever after. We each had our issues, but I know that I was difficult to live with at that time.

Having kids brought me face to face with relationship challenges and my inadequacies as an emotionally healthy person. I was afraid for my children and wanted to protect them so badly.

Even though their dad was safe, I don't think I wanted to have a man in the house while they grew up.

When my ex and I sat down to discuss separating, we wanted to keep the kids' lives as stable as possible. It made sense for their dad to move into an apartment and the kids to stay in the house with me. It was the only place they had ever lived. They were 5 and 3 years old.

We were able to talk calmly even though we were both sad. We were tired of fighting and could see no way past our problems. We had tried counseling too late. It was neither of our faults although we both wanted the other person to change.

It was a kind of relief to call it quits. We were then able to concentrate on what was best for the innocents in the equation. We grew to be great at co-parenting.

Relationships take work, the trick is realizing which ones are worth it. Sometimes the best thing to do is give up. If your safety is an issue or if you can no longer work things out after trying your best, there's no shame in leaving.

It's vital to protect your children from harm. If you have a volatile relationship and they are witnessing things they shouldn't be exposed to, you need to change the situation.

RELATIONSHIPS AND DIVORCE

I don't understand people who get divorced and don't let go of the conflicts. I always say, "That's the beauty of divorce: You don't have to fight anymore. If you want to keep fighting, you should just stay together."

When you call it quits you don't have to try to change the other person, find agreement or understanding. You're giving up on making the marriage work. However, it will be important to find a way to make co-parenting work. You must strive to get along and only deal with matters about the kids.

You'll need to forget about blame and find some forgiveness for each of you about what happened in the marriage. Forgiveness can be tough, but it's a growth experience. Let's explore why and why not to forgive in the next chapter.

Chapter 7

Forgiveness

Forgive and forget. Those are nice words if someone misses a lunch date with you and apologizes. But it's a whole different subject when your parents harmed you when they should've taken care of you. You may forget some of it, but it's very hard to forgive these acts once you accept the ugly truth of what they did to you.

You have unique experiences from childhood and reasons why you may or may not want to forgive. Finding some level of forgiveness enables you to move on. When you free yourself from the internal pain you will be able to be a better parent.

Is it necessary to forgive your abuser? Only you can decide if and when you want to forgive. Here's my journey with forgiveness, and how I have flip-flopped on the idea.

Webster's definition of the word Forgive is: To pardon or absolve. To stop being angry about or resentful against. To give up or let go.

The first part hits me in the anger button. No way am I going to pardon or absolve my father of his crimes against me. I don't condone what he did for years to his daughters or think it's OK in any way. I am also never going to forget about it.

But forgiveness, I learned, wasn't for him. It wasn't even about him. It was for me. I was the one holding on to the anger and hurt for so long. He was happily living his life somewhere.

I can see the value in the second part of the definition of forgive - "To stop being angry about or resentful against. To give up or let go."

The problem with continuing to carry the pain and anger is that it just gets heavier. I was holding so tightly to the pain that it was like taking poison myself – expecting him to get sick.

Pain causes more pain. I needed to think about reframing what forgiveness meant to me. It wasn't an admission that I forgave his acts. It only meant that I was willing to let go of changing the past and wanted to move forward.

You can send forgiveness to someone in your heart and you don't have to share it with them. Then you can find relief within yourself. You can write a letter of forgiveness but never send it. The act of forgiving is for your own peace. You can choose how you want to do it.

My sister, Terrin, told me that holding resentment and anger towards someone keeps you connected to that person. By not forgiving them, you're allowing them to have power over you.

Terrin also explained that she would forgive me of almost anything to keep our relationship intact. But some forgiveness serves to sever a relationship. Such as sending our father on his way with a "I forgive you, bye-bye."

The goal of forgiving your abuser is for you to find peace. You can gain freedom from them continuing to hurt you. You may not have had any choice in the past, but now you can take control and refuse to give them any more of your "head space."

FORGIVENESS

Forgiving My Mother

It took a while for me to forgive my mother. I had harbored so much anger, resentment and frankly, hatred, toward her for way too long. Because of my feeling that she had abandoned and stopped loving me, she was easiest to be mad at.

My father was actually the one who tried to stay engaged with us and helped with homework, drove us places, took us canoeing and to church. He was the person in charge and who we felt dependent on. I didn't hate him as much as I did my mother.

She was weak, angry and only talked to us about what we were doing wrong - so I felt no loyalty to her.

On my way to the bus stop I would step on all the cracks in the sidewalk wondering if it would really break her back. Her abandonment hurt so badly that I wanted to hurt her.

We were never close after I was about 10 years old. It seemed she liked us when we were young and needed her. After we started developing a sense of self and growing away from her, she didn't know how to relate.

It felt like she held us responsible for her marriage problems. She seemed to blame us for our father's behavior and treated us like competition instead of her children. She couldn't make him stop abusing us but seemed angry because we didn't. I'll never understand what was going on in her head.

I came to realize that she was deeply depressed. I don't know if she'd ever had a friend in her life that she could confide in. I don't think she was able to uncover her feelings. It seems that it would've been too much for her to handle.

My heart aches for her now. She was so unhappy and it wasn't fair that she took it out on her daughters. But I can find understanding and compassion for the trap she found herself in.

It would've been very hard for her to leave our father. Impossible.

Her only choice would've been to move us back to Georgia to live with her parents. She didn't seem close to them and it would've been her worst nightmare to live with them.

I don't know much about her childhood except that her brother got all her parents' approval and they were hard people. I remember them with lines on their faces where smiles should have been.

I suspect that she had some form of abuse as a child and then found herself trapped in a similar situation. She wasn't equipped to protect her children. I have a different resolve. Maybe I am strong, in part, because of her weakness.

Forgive Yourself

The most important thing is for you to forgive yourself. What, you say? I didn't do anything wrong. Good, that's great if you truly feel that way. Your inner child may feel differently.

When my therapist mentioned self-forgiveness to me it really resonated. I had so much guilt that I needed to find a way to forgive myself. It doesn't have to make rational sense. My inner child needed me to forgive her. Even though she wasn't to blame, she felt guilty.

I had to forgive myself for being a vulnerable child, for doing what I had to do to survive, for not telling any adult and for keeping up the pretenses for so long. Finding that forgiveness helped me very much. It helped me not to be so hard on myself.

I needed my inner child to forgive me as well. I continued to abuse my inner child when I was an adult, I didn't take good care of her. I promised her that I wouldn't hurt her anymore and I would love her always. This forgiving of self helped to join my adult and child sides as one.

Self-forgiveness turned out to be the deepest forgiveness I could do. While I found some for my father and mother, I couldn't forgive them completely.

Un-Forgiving My Father

While I worked on it in therapy, the subject of forgiveness attached to my father was a struggle. My brain fought against it. I came to understand that I needed to do it for my own sanity.

When I finally forgave him in 2005, it felt good. It had been 14 years since I had any contact with him. I sent him a letter of forgiveness and opened the lines of communication. I told him a little about my family and agreed to meet with him a few years later. All on my own terms.

Then my anger was renewed in 2014 when I was told that he had molested other family members. I could forgive what had happened to me and all that I was robbed of, but I found it impossible to let it go when I heard that he had continued the abuse.

In 2015 I wrote him a letter telling him off and rescinding my forgiveness. This was after the last time I saw him face to face. It was an emotional time at my second oldest sister's funeral. I blame him for much of my late sister's suffering in life. I got angry with him when he kept trying to talk to me when I was avoiding him.

He had followed me outside, away from the crowd. He had genealogy papers to give me and was asking me to tell Terrin he was sorry. He was so needy, and I was so angry at him. I told him that he owed an apology to many more people in the family.

He asked what more he could do and I said, "Don't touch another child!" He's hard of hearing so I had to lean in and yell it using my meanest voice. He snapped back as if I'd struck him, saying "Of course not!"

"I don't believe you" I said flatly. He struggled to explain that it was long ago and admitted that "it was a terrible obsession." I was just getting madder at him. Someone came and pulled me away, asking if I was all right. "I'm OK, I'm strong because of that MotherF-er."

That was the last thing I said to him and it left us both shaken. He just doesn't get it. To him, the abuse is something from the past that doesn't fit in his present. To me, it's pain put upon me that has affected my entire life. Maybe he'll read this book and gain an inkling of how devastating child molesting really is for children. I doubt it.

I don't expect anything from him. I don't wish to see him or speak to him again. I am done. He sends me a birthday or Christmas card every year. I don't respond.

Maybe I'll find forgiveness again someday. Right now, it feels good to be angry even though I know it doesn't hurt him.

I live most of my days without giving him another thought. My best revenge is living a happy life.

So, the moral of my story is: find forgiveness for your own well-being – or not. Only you can decide if it's a good idea for

FORGIVENESS

you. Either way, I hope that you continue your healing and work on becoming the shining light in the world that you are meant to be.

PART 2

RAISING GOOD KIDS

Introduction

You are your child's first love. They adore you and look to you for their validation. They delight in your smiles and making you laugh. See yourself through their eyes. Be silly, laugh more, play and enjoy the little things. Forget the crappy treatment you got and enjoy a happy childhood along with your children.

It is a constant job when kids are little to figure out what they need. They need a lot of guidance. You need to be tuned in and not tuned out. Your job is to be available for your kids.

You must rise to the challenge. Your kids are watching. It's impossible to teach them to be honest if you aren't. If you expect them to be considerate, clean, responsible and kind – then you must model it for them. Consider what qualities you want your kids to have and make damn sure you show them those traits yourself.

No one's perfect and parenting points it out to you time after time. There's nothing that will challenge you more to be a better person. That's the golden prize. For all your dedication to your children's needs instead of your own, you will be a better person.

Much of parenting is done on the fly – at the crucial moment that someone is falling out of a tree or has just dropped the jar of pickles on the floor – and you react. There's no time to stop, think, and respond in a rational manner. That would be nice. In day-to-day life with little heathens – you get angry, frustrated, overwhelmed, scared, fed up, exhausted and many other feelings of defeat.

PARENTING WELL AFTER CHILDHOOD ABUSE

Each childhood stage brings its new and frustrating challenges. You don't have to worry about what's coming down the line, just take care of now. Try to be present and learn what you need to know at this point. Do your best at each stage. Effective parenting is learned along the way.

It's important to remember that there will be a natural end to each phase. Children are growing up and testing us through the journey. Remember: "When you're going through hell. Just keep going."

Luckily the little buggers are so cute and adorable in between their frustrating antics, that you can stand them when it gets tough. The cute and cuddly times are the reward for the hard work and self-restraint you will have to practice over and over. Keep going – "practice makes good enough." Remember, nobody's perfect.

You may see some other parents who make it look easy, who have patience by the bucket load. It's an illusion. Somewhere, sometimes, they go crazy too. The trick that survivors must learn, that our parents didn't have, is the restraint part. We cannot afford to lose it to a breaking point.

Survivors must find the mature way to handle things and remember to focus on showing respect and dignity to their children. When we are healthier minded our reactions will be healthier.

It's not fair to compare our children or ourselves to others, but everyone does it. If you know someone who seems to have it together, ask them how they do it. You may find out they have wine in that coffee cup.

Try to imitate the attitudes of parents you think are doing it right. I learned a lot from parents on sitcoms like, "Growing Pains." The dad seemed to have all the answers. Of course, they were written for him by the writers.

INTRODUCTION

Search for parenting tips. There are a million articles about parenting on the internet. There are probably specific answers to your questions. You don't have to "reinvent the wheel."

There's no shame in asking for advice or expressing that you need help. Give yourself a break. In order to be nicer to your children you need to practice being nicer to yourself. It'll probably take a lot of practice.

When you're a survivor of child abuse, unhealthy ways of reacting to stressful situations may get in the way of effective parenting. While you're healing yourself, you must practice self-awareness and try not to overreact to the current situation.

It's not always easy to know where to start. In this section I'll share some of my experiences and lessons learned in raising my own incredible children.

Chapter 1
Children's Bill of Rights

Every newborn should come to us with a note like this:

> "What you have just been given is a gift from above. You are instructed to treat it with the utmost care – now and each day that it is in your charge." —God

From my experience from a child abuse victim to a survivor, and all the healing work done in between, I've created a Children's Bill of Rights.

1. All children should feel secure that their basic needs of food, clothing and shelter will be met.

This sounds like a "no brainer", but neglect is one of the ways children are abused every day. If the parents are unstable in their lives, due to drugs, mental illness or being unable to keep a job; then they won't be taking care of the basic needs of their family. There's not enough money for everything and their priorities may be messed up.

When kids have to go to school hungry, be embarrassed about worn out clothes and worry about the electricity being turned off; their self-esteem is being damaged. They can't function as well as they have a right to. Children deserve a sense of security.

2. All children deserve to be nurtured and given positive feelings about themselves.

Children deserve the freedom to be themselves and engage in creative play. Try not to judge them about being as you expect them to be. Is it OK if your girl is loud and wants to play drums, while your boy would rather read than play sports? Accept and encourage the strengths of each individual child.

3. All children deserve to be respected and their feelings considered.

Their feelings should be treated with tenderness and compassion. When reprimanding them, remember to keep their dignity intact. Don't call them names.

4. A child's best interest should always come first.

Parents must put their own wishes aside when making decisions involving their children. The kids' needs come first. When there is a choice to be made – "what's best for the children?" is the deciding factor.

5. All children's innocence should be protected from exposure to inappropriate language and entertainment

When children are exposed to violence or sexual scenes at an early age it's confusing; at the least, and damaging, at the worst. Once they see something (as in graphic violence) it goes into the subconscious mind and cannot be erased.

When making entertainment choices, adults should consider what's appropriate for the children. Even when they are "too young to understand", children don't need to be exposed to sex or frightening images.

Most parents will use bad language occasionally, it comes with the job. However, if you cuss directly at a child and call them names, you need to examine where your anger is coming from and stop yourself. If others are using offensive language around your children you can say, "Language. Please stop talking like that around the kids or we will have to leave."

The harmful, inappropriate talk is more insidious in our culture: Uncle Joey saying "Oh yeah, I'd do her – and her sister" when watching a TV show. This objectifying of women teaches boys and girls that anyone can "do" what they want to them.

People are so used to hearing degrading comments about females that it's passed over as joking – nobody means anything hurtful. This thinking needs to be challenged. It's harmful – especially to children who are gathering information like sponges.

6. All children should be able to trust adults to be honest.

It sure would be nice if children could keep their innocence and trust all adults to treat them fairly. As their parent you must be someone they can trust completely to be safe and not harmful.

PARENTING WELL AFTER CHILDHOOD ABUSE

It's the job of adults to shield children from the harsh realities of life. We need to keep explanations age appropriate about troubling subjects in the news but strive to be honest as much as possible.

Children are watching and listening all the time. They will learn to be truth tellers or liars from the adults around them.

If your parents were abusive you were probably taught to lie. To be a better parent, it's important to foster honesty with your children.

Chapter 2

Honesty is the Best Policy

When I was in sixth grade, I tried to be honest with my mother and she got mad and shot me down. I begged her not to tell my dad if I told her a secret and she promised that she wouldn't. After I confessed that I had skipped school she immediately yelled for my father, "Daddy! Come in here and hear what this little girl did today."

I could not believe she betrayed me. I learned that I couldn't trust her, that she would tell my dad everything, and she certainly was not strong enough to handle my biggest secret. I didn't try to confide in her again.

As a survivor, have you asked yourself what if your parents would have been safe to talk to? How would your life have been different? Most likely you didn't often experience open and honest communication in your family. Where there's abuse, there are secrets, and lying becomes the norm.

I worked hard to change that cycle for my children's sake. Because I couldn't be honest when I was a child, it was important to have honesty in my children's home. I wanted my children to trust me and to feel safe. I especially wanted them to be able to tell me if anyone was hurting them. I wanted them to feel that I would be on their side and be their champion in all situations.

I wanted my kids to feel that they could tell me absolutely ANYTHING. Which meant that I had to listen and try to withhold judgement on what they told me. I tried to be curious and ask questions (even when I thought I knew the answers) to help them figure out their own solutions.

When a child does something wrong their first reaction may be to say, "I didn't do it." You don't want them to be scared to admit when they have made a mistake. Ideally, you want them to come and tell you when something happens, apologize and then help to clean it up.

What if your anger makes your child hide things from you? How angry would you be to find poopy pants at the bottom of the clothes hamper? Oh, it could happen. Even if you build a code of trust and tell your kids it's safe to tell you anything, they may still hide things from you. Hopefully not the big things. Establishing a policy of trust and acceptance is crucial to developing honest relationships.

If your goal is to promote honesty, then you need to let confessions lead to solutions and not punishment.

I always told my children that telling the truth may make me mad, but it wouldn't get them into trouble. I had to stick by that. I wanted to raise honest kids. Telling the truth is hard to do when you're admitting that you made a mistake. By my encouraging them to confess, with promise of no punishment, I taught them that feeling of relief when the truth is told, and the consequence is acceptance. Think about that for a minute.

You know how hard it is to confess a lie or admit that you made a mistake? Holding these things in feels bad and you worry about the consequence if someone finds out. What if you could feel safe telling the truth and the outcome was that your boss, partner or friend says, "Wow, OK. I'm glad you told me. Let's figure out how to fix this."

HONESTY IS THE BEST POLICY

Of course, you can feel mad if your child spills grape juice on the rug. You can go to your room and cuss about it. Yes, it needs to be cleaned but it can wait for you to calm down. If you start soaking it up when you're mad, you may say something hurtful. "What the hell? Can't you hold onto your cup? Why did you have grape juice in this room anyway?" Blame, shame, blame. Not productive.

You could say, "Argh!, I'm glad you told me about the mess but I'm feeling mad about it. I know it was an accident. I'm going to be by myself until I get over it. Then you can help me clean it up."

While in your room you can realize that your darling children are much more valuable than any rug. You can feel good about modelling appropriate behavior when someone you love gives you bad news, like spilled grape juice. Truth is Love.

Kids are listening to what you say and learning how to act by watching your actions. One of my pet peeves is hearing the "white lies" that get told to children by unthinking parents.

Dad tells the boys "Don't tell your mom" when getting ice cream before dinner. Sure, it's a seemingly harmless thing to do. But the subtle messages are that you don't have to be honest, it's OK to keep secrets, and mom is not respected enough to know the truth. Not good messages.

Couldn't a dad honestly say, "Don't tell your mom we had ice cream. Ha-ha, just kidding, we don't keep secrets in this family."? The kids may or may not mention it to their mom, and the dad is strong enough to handle the consequences. He's showing the children that mommy and daddy have an honest relationship.

If you grew up in an environment of secrets and lies, you already value honesty a great deal. The damage that

PARENTING WELL AFTER CHILDHOOD ABUSE

dishonesty has done in your life can be changed. Living in truth will heal you and make you a great parent.

Chapter 3
The Power of Apology

Being honest sometimes means that you'll have to apologize.

While you're working on yourself it's nice to have these loving little people around to make you feel better. They love you, they need you and they will forgive you almost anything. So, don't be afraid to be honest and apologize if you make a mistake. Overreacting in anger was something I had to apologize to my kids for often.

The one thing my parents never did was apologize to me when I was young. Their word was the law. We obeyed because they "said so". No reasoning and no right to know why.

My parents didn't show us respect and we didn't respect them. We only feared their authority. Kids are smart, and while they aren't always able to reason things out, it shows you respect their feelings when you explain things to them.

Sometimes your kids will confront you with your own contradictions in rule-following. "But mom, you took the last roll without asking!" (One of my rules when you are sharing food is to ask before you take the last one of something.)

It's OK – in fact, good – for your kids to see that you make mistakes and forget the rules sometimes too. If you show your humanness, then it lets them feel less pressure to be perfect all the time. This is a good time to model what to do when you make a mistake. "Oops, I guess I did do that. I wasn't thinking. I'm sorry. I'll try to do better."

That's a problem I had with my parents' totalitarian style, they never admitted they were wrong. It was as if we were supposed to believe they were perfect, when we could clearly see that they were not time after time. They lost all credibility. When they were wrong, we were not supposed to notice. They expected their stupid rules to be followed because they were in charge and we were the "pee-ons" with no other choice.

I encourage you to show – not weakness – but your humanness to your children. This will help them accept themselves and have compassion for others for being fallible. When you make a mistake, say you're sorry. Apologizing is a way of taking responsibility for your words and actions.

"Madeline, I'm sorry I forgot to put a peach in your lunchbox like you asked. I hope you weren't too disappointed." This gives her the fantastic opportunity to be the bigger person and say, "It's OK, mommy, maybe you'll remember tomorrow."

Asking for forgiveness for large and small things is a great skill to model. I believe it builds respect and closeness between people.

When I got overwhelmed and yelled at my children, reacting too harshly to whatever mess they made, I would feel very sorry once I had calmed down. Instead of just feeling badly, I would take the opportunity to go to them with a heartfelt apology. They always said it was OK and they forgave me. I tried to always place the blame on myself for overreacting, not bringing up what they did, so it was a true apology.

The following scenario is not a true apology:

THE POWER OF APOLOGY

"Robbie, sweetheart. I'm so sorry for losing it and yelling at you earlier, but you made me so mad when you wrote all over your door! Do you know how expensive doors are? I'm going to have to hire someone to put up a new one or you'll just have marker all over your door until college."

This apology started out on the right track, then descended into blame. Robbie probably won't hear a heartfelt apology. He will be focused on trying to figure out how much a door costs and how he made you overreact. He will think that he's responsible for your actions and feelings. That's not true, adults are responsible for their own feelings and actions.

You must be careful not to place blame on your child for "making" you react badly.

No one causes anyone else's behavior. Your reactions are your choice. The act of apologizing should not be a cover to do something over and over. "I'm sorry" means you learned a lesson to not act the same way. It's an opportunity to say "I will do better. I will try not to do that again."

Let's get back to the earlier scenario where 6-year-old Robbie wrote big black lines all over his bedroom door. You completely lost it; yelling at him, maybe cussing and making him cry. You have given yourself a time out, done some breathing and tried to put it in perspective. The mess was made, and everyone is sorry.

Your apologizing for your reaction doesn't make it OK for him to deface property, but you want to let him know that you don't like the way you handled it.

"Sweetie, (hug) I'm so sorry for how I acted earlier. I shouldn't have yelled and pushed you into your room. I know it scared you and I don't want to hurt you. Can you forgive me?"

See how this didn't bring up what he did? Everyone is well aware of what happened. What you're addressing is that yelling and hurting are not acceptable ways to deal with things that make you angry.

Do you want your kid to yell and kick the dog when it doesn't listen to him? Then you must show him another way. With practice it could go like this: "Oh no! Robbie, what the heck were you thinking?" Taking away the marker... "We don't write on the house! That's what paper is for." "Ooh, I am so mad right now, I am going to my room, and you stay in yours."

Milk spills, kids write on stuff, things break, – but that's just "what happened". Practice taking a breath and accepting that mistakes are going to happen. Teach your kids that you can clean it up, glue it back together, and apologize if you hurt someone's feelings.

Here are some examples of apologizing without taking blame: "I'm sorry you had a bad day." "I'm sorry you don't like what I said." "I'm sorry you dropped your ice cream cone." None of these take on responsibility but convey that you were listening and have sympathy for their feelings.

I tried to feel good about apologizing around my kids. It conveyed that I made mistakes but took responsibility for them. I hoped this made my children realize it was OK to make their own mistakes and occasionally mess up royally.

How can we expect children to do everything right? They are literally beginners in this life. Sometimes the message we send is that they're unlovable and disappointing to us if they aren't perfect. What if we allowed them to make mistakes and be human without feeling terrible about it? They can learn the magic of saying "I'm sorry" when they mess up.

THE POWER OF APOLOGY

There's empowerment in asking for forgiveness. Asking "can you forgive me?" shows that you're sorry for causing stress and gives the receiver the chance to contemplate whether it's forgivable. It gives them the power to let it go.

The next chapter explores ways to empower your children by having realistic expectations and accepting all of their feelings.

Chapter 4
Managing Expectations. Accepting Feelings

Kids will live up or down to your expectations. When I heard this advice, I realized that I needed to examine my expectations. I wanted to hold my children to a high standard of behaving, with good morals and decency. I expected them to do their best in everything they tried. I had hopes that they would to go to college, but I always told them that I expected it.

What I needed to learn was how to hold them to high standards while letting them make mistakes. How to keep my expectations high while not being overly controlling of outcomes. I wanted them to gain confidence by not expecting excellence in all things.

Disappointments happen in life. You'll be disappointed in yourself, your friend, your coworker, your lover and your child. This is due to humans having expectations of how things will turn out. The real problem is in expecting people to act the way you want them to. That's a set up to be let down.

People – and yes, children are people – will not act the way you want them to a lot of the time. This is a big problem with kids, they just go off script. Even when you tell them, "Now I want you to be very quiet while I get some work done" or "Timmy, do not pick your nose in church", children will likely do the exact opposite. They can't help it and you mustn't get too mad because they are "in training".

It's a child's right to act childish. You can expect them to make messes, break things and misbehave at the worst moments. It's the parent's tough job to handle their kids' mistakes and deal with them in a rational manner.

It was your parent's responsibility to teach you how to behave when "stuff happened", i.e. "you clean it up" – without punching you in the face, screaming obscenities at you, rubbing your face in the mess, cutting you with glass or any of the other horrible extremes that some adults have gone to.

They may have thought that they were teaching you a lesson, but the lesson learned was that they were to be feared and you were incapable of pleasing them. Which is why you felt it was all your fault – but it absolutely wasn't. As a child you were predictably going to make mistakes.

If your parents were physically abusive you may have been told it was your own fault. If you weren't so bad, they wouldn't have to hurt you. Violence is not discipline.

I learned that discipline is different than punishment. My parents had rules and if you broke them, you were punished. There were lectures but not reasonable discussions. My father's choice was the rule of law.

The problem with punishment is that the outcome of changing behavior is rarely achieved. The child just learns how to do what they want and not get caught. One thing that works is positive reinforcement and a rewards system for good behavior. There are many books on discipline.

Humans fail and young ones should get a pass to do it often. It's kind of their job. They are born into this great big world not knowing how to do anything and must be guided by their elders. Parents are patient with babies and think it's so cute when they make a mess or wobble around. They get older

MANAGING EXPECTATIONS. ACCEPTING FEELINGS

and are expected to know how to do things better, not make mistakes, and clean up after themselves?

Let's be more realistic. Don't expect that they will perform daily the way you think they should. Remember that they will turn out fine even if they're imperfect at things right now.

Unfortunately, some parents don't believe in their kids' abilities enough. Maybe there have been some struggles in school or with social behavior, but these things shouldn't make a parent give up hope for improvement. Some parents have very low expectations of what their kids are capable of accomplishing. This leads to doing more things for them than necessary, running interference and not helping them to believe in themselves.

I've seen this with some friends who have done everything for their son hoping that he will gain independence one day. They don't teach him household skills because they don't expect him to help around the house. They try to fix every problem and shield him from responsibility because they don't believe he can handle failure.

Failure can be a great teacher. It teaches resilience. What will happen in the future? Their son will always rely on his parents? How will he learn to unclog a drain, get his car fixed, make a doctor appointment, handle losing a job?

My friend hurt his back picking up a yard full of tree limbs after a storm. I asked if his teenage son was there to help and was told "No, he wasn't awake." By not asking his son to pitch in, the expectation was set that the teen wasn't capable of being helpful. The dad would rather hurt himself than have his son grumble at him about doing a chore.

Low expectations hurt children's self-esteem. It doesn't help them when they need to work for someone. Even if they grumble about having to do yardwork, deep down it gives them a sense of belonging and added value to the family.

Expectations are a balancing act. You want to promote confidence by expecting hard work and success. You don't want to be inflexible and too hard on them though. When trying to set realistic expectations of your kids there are two rules to live by: 1. Some days will be better than others. 2. Always try to do your best.

This is a great thing to remember as parents – that we try to do our best and will fail sometimes. Accept this about yourself and say it to your kids, "Everyone makes mistakes."

While unrealistic expectations can be a bad idea and bring you disappointment, it's necessary to have realistic ones for your children. At school age, they have many challenges and you must be there to encourage and help them through the tough times. Show them how to manage their feelings about struggles. By definition children are immature. They will struggle with homework, getting along with their peers and their confusing feelings about everything.

Accepting Feelings

Can you remember what it felt like to be a kid? It's overwhelming not to be in control of anything while not understanding how the world works. Kids are confused about the tides of emotions coursing through their bodies – long before puberty.

One of the greatest gifts you can give your kids when they are small (toddler age) are the words for feelings. You tell them what a fire truck is and what to call it – you also need to teach them the things they can't see but are feeling.

MANAGING EXPECTATIONS. ACCEPTING FEELINGS

Children tend to go in and out of feeling emotions deeply without realizing what's happening. What if we gave them a word for how they're feeling so they can express it and feel better?

For example, your 2-year-old is rolling on the floor screaming because their balloon burst and you sigh and say, "Honey, I'm sorry your balloon popped, you must be so sad. You really were having fun playing with it."

This shows them that you understand the feeling of being sad when you really enjoyed something and then it's over. You're not treating them as acting crazy over a small thing, but rather showing that you see their feeling of sadness and it's OK.

Even though you know you can solve the problem for them, you give it a minute to allow them to be sad about the broken toy. It's very valuable to teach the acceptance of feelings and allowing them to pass.

Of course, if the screaming gets worse or carries on, you can excuse yourself without trying to stop their expression, "Jeez, you really are upset. I'm going to be in my room (or send them to their room) and you let me know when you are done crying. OK?"

In this same scenario you may be tempted to use reason and problem solving – but it won't show empathy and teach about dealing with feelings. You may say "Honey, I'm sorry your balloon broke but you were hitting it against the table. Stop crying, we'll just blow up another one." If you brush off the crying and move on by replacing the broken toy – you're teaching that bad feelings are to be ignored, shut down and avoided. You must fix them immediately.

Life can be challenging. Being able to name feelings and work through emotions instead of stuffing them inside will make for happier and healthier lives.

Little boys are often taught to deny their feelings, not to cry and to "man up". This is not doing them any favors in dealing with normal feelings. Their hidden pain can turn into expressions of anger.

Girls are often taught it's not OK to be angry or express "negative" feelings – they're liked better if they are compliant and quiet. Try to allow both boys and girls to accept and express their feelings.

Steps in dealing with feelings:

- See the Reaction
- Name the Feeling
- Acknowledge that they feel it
- Watch it pass
- Move on to problem solving

When moving too quickly from step one (see someone crying) to solving the problem for them (new balloon) they miss the lesson of allowing feelings and feeling understood. Children need to learn that feelings aren't bad and they can deal with them. Even the worst – death of a loved one – can be dealt with without losing your mind or dying yourself.

Watching your child experience intense feelings can be tough. But in the long run it's crucial for their happiness to see feelings as normal. I don't know about you; but I feel that

MANAGING EXPECTATIONS. ACCEPTING FEELINGS

you must know sadness to really know joy and you need darkness to appreciate light.

Doesn't it always feel better when you let your feelings out instead of holding onto them or being confused by them? If we all had the names for emotions wouldn't it make it easier to figure out which one you're feeling and release it?

It's sometimes hard to remain calm in situations where your child is out of control and "losing it", but it's important to try. You can diffuse an escalation by not reacting and try instead to help them regain control of themselves.

Let's say you're in a store with your three-year-old daughter and she suddenly throws herself on the floor and screams "Waaah, you're mean."

You have to be in charge. Instead of yanking her up and dragging her away; take a deep breath, "Honey, I can see that you're very upset that we have to leave the toy area. You're sad and disappointed. I understand. You can be sad, but we can't stay here all afternoon. How about a hug and some deep breaths to calm down?" You may be in a hurry, but it only takes a minute for you to understand where she's coming from and accept her feeling.

It's OK for your child to be upset sometimes. Negative feelings don't have to be scary. Don't we want our children to learn to handle their emotions? They can learn early that feelings come and go. The intensity doesn't last long, especially if they're understood.

Here are some feeling words you can use to help identify what your child may be feeling.

Angry, Sad, Happy, Excited, Proud, Disappointed, Frustrated, Afraid, Confused, Tired and Hungry.

PARENTING WELL AFTER CHILDHOOD ABUSE

Our children can learn to tune into their feelings and to express them appropriately. Early on we train them to notice the signals that they must go to the bathroom so they can make it without an accident. This is a very important life skill. So is identifying how they're feeling.

Instead of just saying "Stop that", helping your child explore their feeling can teach them to learn to control that feeling in the future. You can see the relief in a toddler's face when you name what they're feeling,

"It looks like you are very frustrated with that puzzle piece right now"

Banging the table, he scowls "Yeth, I am fwustated." He feels understood.

"It's a new puzzle and I understand if you're frustrated with it." You've acknowledged that he feels it.

"OK, do you want to keep trying? I know you can do it. Or do you want to take a break and come back to it later?" He learns there are options to deal with the feeling.

You have just given your child permission to feel their frustration and a way to get past it. If they're throwing the puzzle pieces at their brother, you can say "Hey, why are you angry at the puzzle? Are you frustrated that it's not fitting? Don't throw it at your brother. Maybe you need a break."

Toddlers and teenagers are similar in their over-reactions to their feelings. It's good to remember the "labelling feelings" tactic later when the hormones set in.

When your preteen gets an attitude you can say, "I see that you're angry that you can't play video games until you do your homework. That's OK. I understand. You can be angry, but the sooner you get your work done the sooner you can play."

MANAGING EXPECTATIONS. ACCEPTING FEELINGS

Be matter-of-fact. Of course, you understand frustration and anger. Tell them "I understand" but it doesn't change the rule. Everyone gets angry, but it's important to learn how to express it appropriately.

Have you ever trained a dog to obey you? You learn to use different voices to convey your meaning. A high-pitched tone means, "It's time to play. Come here. Let's go." You must find your lower, serious voice when you want to get their attention, "Come here right now. No! Stop that."

When you want to be taken seriously by your child you don't have to be mean, but firm and in charge. There's a difference between barking "You stay in your room until it's spotless" in your loud, mean tone – and remaining calm saying matter-of-factly, "When I come back in one hour, I expect to see this room straightened."

You can't be your child's best friend. It's not your job to make them happy all the time. It's your job to protect them and to teach them how to behave. Once you have taught them how to deal with their own feelings, you can practice letting them do it.

When you're the parent you must make decisions and uphold rules that may make you unpopular with your kids. The next chapter will show you why it's important to do it anyway.

Chapter 5
Who's in Charge?

If you're struggling to overcome childhood abuse, you may not feel like an adult at times. With a kid to take care of, you must catch up quickly. Remember, you're now a parent and must be the adult.

You now must learn the definitions of responsibility, selflessness, self-awareness and caretaking. It's no longer acceptable for you to be the needy one, the one who always gets their way or the one without consequences. Because now there will be direct consequences to everything you do to your kids.

It's not a child's job to think about other people's needs or feelings. They are takers when they're small, and parents are supposed to be the givers. When parents are immature themselves or don't consider this natural role process, they can be resentful and try to force the kids to be more considerate of their needs. Ha! What a set up for disappointment.

Parents absolutely must consider life from their kid's perspective and realize that their needs come first. It's only fair. Every choice and decision needs to be made with the thought of what's best for the kids.

Just because it's all about the kids – doesn't mean that you give them everything and your only job is to make them happy. That's not true at all. You can try to say "Yes" more than "No" – but you absolutely are responsible for training them to be polite and thoughtful of others, how to act in public, how to do everything basically.

You've just been put in charge of a wild animal and you have 16-18 years to train it. Loving them is a balance of making them feel like the center of the universe and teaching them that everyone else is that too.

Being a parent means that you're responsible for your children's protection, nurturing, safety, house rules, education, health, emotional well-being and the list goes on and on. You're the person in charge. You get to decide how you want to parent. This will be an ever-changing process as children grow and their needs change.

Your kids need you to make the decisions for them while they're small. Your choices teach them how to make decisions for themselves. Your decisions provide guidelines and structure that kids need in order to feel secure.

Kids who are given too much authority over themselves can feel insecure, because they know that they aren't equipped to be in charge. Children need rules, guidance and boundaries to be set by their parents.

You want to foster closeness with your kids but can you be best friends with them? No, experts agree that children need parents to be parents. You need to be the parent and make the tough decisions. It's not an egalitarian setup.

Children will have friends, but they only have you to be their parent. You should have fun with them, support and encourage them as a friend would. But when they do something wrong, must be held to task or need guidance it's your job to do it. Not their friends.

What about the parents who let their kids decide everything? Giving too much responsibility to children is not kind. Some kids have been led to believe they can be in charge. Their parent may feel guilty about divorce and afraid to upset their child at all costs. A parent who is otherwise strong and responsible lets their kid run all over them, even asking permission from them. "I'd like you to turn off the video game at 11 pm tonight, OK?"

Remember not to say, "OK?" When you say a rule, don't ask for their permission. If you feel like you need their validation, then you aren't thinking like the parent they need you to be. You're responsible for knowing what's best for them. They don't have to like your rules or decisions.

How hard is it to take a deep breath, find your backbone and say,"Hey buddy, game off at 11:00, got it?" Don't ask – tell. Matter of fact. In the case of video or computer time you'll have to go back at the deadline and tell them it's time. It's unreasonable to think they will watch the clock. Hint: You can set your wifi to turn off at a certain time.

Once you have done this a few dozen times though, they'll know that what you say is what will happen, and they may become clock watchers on their own. Fingers-crossed.

Of course, you don't have to be a dictator. As they get older it's appropriate to engage children in more decisions. When you do let your kids decide, you better be ready to accept their choice. I suggest giving them two or three acceptable choices.

For instance, if you have limited money to spend, don't ask them what they want to do this weekend. That's too broad of a choice. They may pick Disney World or shopping at the mall. You can say "I was thinking about going to the movies this weekend or would you rather go out to dinner?"

Consistency

It's important to be consistent with your promises and your rules. While raising kids, being consistent means you're going to be someone they can count on. Your word means something. If you're wishy washy, they will lose respect for you and won't feel secure. We don't need any more insecure people in the world.

Consistency is where a lot of parents screw up. If a rule is important to you, then you need to be vigilant to make sure it is followed. You have to pick your battles. You can't fight over every little thing your kid does that you don't like. This may have been what your controlling parents did to you. Let the small stuff slide.

Enforcing important rules is where your strength and fortitude come in. You can do it. You're wiser and more skilled than the young ones. They will go for the chink in your armor if you show inconsistency in what you say or do.

If one of your house rules is washing your hands before you eat, then you must tell them at each meal until they get it. You must wash your own hands every time. Kids are watching you and will model what you do more often than what you say.

Here's an example of making a rule that you don't feel like seeing through. At dinner you say, "You can't have any pudding until you eat all of your meat." One child pushes meat around the plate, leaving most of it. You feel badly serving pudding to everyone else except your little vegetarian, and give in. You say "well, next time you won't get dessert if you don't eat all your dinner."

Everyone knows that the child won that battle. As the words are coming out of your mouth you know that it isn't true. You will probably cave in the next time too. You might as well save your breath and not say that they can't have pudding. This is obviously not an important rule for you.

If a rule is important, then you must take a hard line and stand your ground. It's OK if your child cries over a consequence, it's a good lesson. Lessons are learned by making mistakes. They chose not to eat dinner and didn't get dessert. They had a choice. It's good to remind them of that fact.

By supporting the rule, you're teaching them to think the next time you give them a choice, because you will uphold your words. By making rules that you care enough to enforce – you're saving the world from one more selfish person who thinks they can have things their way without rules applying to them. Good for you.

Your being in charge is not the same as being a dictator. You can be firm in your rules without being mean. Likewise, you don't want to go the other extreme of your parents (if they were hard and ruled by intimidation) by becoming a pushover, with a spine of mush. Snap out of it! You must have fortitude and a strong backbone to get through this. Kids will see weakness and pounce on it. They will take advantage of your breaking a rule and you'll have to start back at square one to show them that you mean what you say.

It's also important to keep your promises. Kids never forget that you didn't do it one time when you said that you would. Their job is to test you and they are very good at their job.

Who's Responsible for the Kids?

Parenting is not all fun and games, unless you have full-time nannies and caretakers for your kids. Perhaps you only have your children brought to you when they are clean, fed and have been taught manners. You don't share in the day to day upkeep and have them taken away if they annoy you. I've seen this in movies, like the "Sound of Music" but it's not how most families work these days.

It's old-fashioned, but some dads are not expected to contribute in the day to day care of their children. One mom raves about her husband, "Oh, Dan's such a good dad. He plays ball with the kids every evening before dinner." That's nice of Dan, but does he help with dinner, bath time, homework, getting everything ready for school the next day?

Managing tasks around a home and children is increasingly more balanced between partners. If you need more help, be sure to ask. Don't assume that your partner won't be more helpful if they aren't even aware of the need.

Nobody is a mind reader. Most people need concrete requests to know what's expected of them. Don't get caught up in thinking that "my partner sees me doing everything, surely they know that I need help." This belief can cause resentment and isn't fair. If you ask directly and your partner refuses to help, then you have cause to resent it. You should probably get some counseling and discuss each of your expectations of parenting roles.

Maybe you were raised by a selfish parent whose needs were always more important than yours. This can be very lonely and hurtful for a child. You didn't ask to be born into their world to "mess it up." Since they had you, they needed to take responsibility and grow up.

No matter what your parents did – it's like the spilled milk – it happened, and now someone needs to clean it up. As you heal and want to change things in your life, you can choose to look at things that happened in a different light. It's now your turn to clean up your own life.

WHO'S IN CHARGE?

That may sound over simplified, but deep down it's the truth. Our upbringing caused us pain and it's not easy to heal. But blaming our actions now on what happened in childhood isn't fair to ourselves or our children. We can become better people, partners and parents. It's no one else's job to heal us. But we don't have to feel alone. Other adults are there to support and love us through our breakdowns and breakthroughs.

Chapter 6

Random Parenting Advice

There are many things that I learned from other parents, books and television shows about parenting effectively. Here are my thoughts about what worked for me and my family.

Communication and Listening to Kids

Two things kids want are to be heard and understood. Doesn't everyone? The reason small children say things over and over is because they want to be acknowledged. You don't have to instantly jump to their request if you're busy. But if you want them to stop asking, you may as well take a second to say that you hear them.

Your child repeats, "I want a cookie, mommy, mommy, cookie, I want a cookie, mom, can I please have a cookie?"

It's fair to tell them why they can't have a cookie right now. Instead of just saying "no". Take an extra minute to acknowledge their request and then tell them why not. It goes like this:

"Sweetie, honeypie, I hear you. You want a cookie and I appreciate you asking so nicely. But you can't have it right now because it's time for breakfast. Cookies are for later."

"But I want a cookie now! Please? Daddy let me have one yesterday morning."

You take a deep breath and decide what you are willing to allow. "Ha-ha, that daddy. Well, I'm your mom and I say you can have 2 cookies - after your nap."

Of course, you have to "pick your battles". If you really don't care if Elijah has a cookie, then try to use it to get something that you want. (Shh, this is a secret parental weapon). When they come to you with a request and it's something you know they really want: Use it to your advantage! It can be a win-win situation.

"Oh, I hear that you want a cookie. Well…" pause for affect, like you have to consider if they deserve it or not…" I suppose you can have one – IF… you don't ask for another thing until lunchtime… after you pick up all these toys.. when you get your homework done… after you draw me a bath." Whatever thing is immediate and that you thought you would have to do yourself or bribe them to do.

Bribery is a fine tactic occasionally. "Use what they want to get what you want". Not every time though. Sometimes give them the cookie, like daddy did, just to see them happy.

It's not always about teaching a lesson, but when you aren't exhausted and get the opportunity to use the win-win tool it can feel very gratifying. You have just taught them consideration for others, that in order to get what they want they sometimes must give back.

Manners and Talking About Your Kids

There are many sides to everyone. It seems we only show our worst ones to our family members. People who are closest to us get the full spectrum of who we are. Nuts, bolts and ugly.

It's in our homes that we feel free to express the full range of our emotions. Children do this too. That's why they seem to fall apart with their parents, when they can behave just fine at school or at a friend's house. That's one goal of parenting: to have your kids know how to behave when they're around other people.

Have you had friends tell you that your child is so polite and well-mannered at their house? You think, "Henry? Are we talking about the same kid?" But inside you can be proud that little Hank has absorbed your lessons and knows when to use them. You may not get to see these manners in everyday life at home.

When you get a chance, be sure to tell him what the neighbor said about him. Kids need to hear compliments and it warms their heart (as it does to all of us) to find out people are talking nicely about them.

I realized one day that I often talked about my kids and said glowing things about them that they never got to hear. I made an effort to throw it into conversation with them. "You know my client, Cheryl, was asking about you and I bragged about how good you're doing on the swim team. I told her how well you did at Saturday's meet. I also said you are eating us out of house and home."

Telling your kids that you're proud of them and how much you love them is great. Hearing you say it to other people is life-affirming and raises their self-esteem.

Teachable Moments

You are your child's first teacher and you will have many opportunities to mold them into loving, respectful, nice people. These times are "teachable moments." Look for these chances in conversations, while watching TV together, when riding in the car and always when they come to you asking for help. Whether it's how to tie their shoe, someone has their toy, their TV idol makes a mistake or what does racism mean? ...you know, life.

Look for chances to teach them your values and to explore what they're thinking. Don't be afraid to say, "I don't know, or I'll have to think about that and get back to you."

What were you taught by your parents? Even in horrible situations there are usually some good things to remember. Mine did a good job teaching me to appreciate music and art, to love nature and animals, as well as how to be cruel and selfish.

In many ways my childhood was good. I loved bike riding and swimming in our pool. My neighborhood was full of kids who would play outside from morning to dinnertime, stopping for lunch and to drink out of the water hose. I had many pets and was grateful for their unconditional love. It was not all darkness.

On the following page is my questionnaire for you to use to explore some of the good things your parents gave you and what you want to change. Take your time and let yourself write whatever comes up first. This is for you – it won't be graded. Be sure to hug your kids when you're done.

I asked friends who were abused, neglected, or had parents with alcoholism and mental illness to give me their feedback. The consensus was that they needed to change A LOT about how they were raised. Here are some of their answers:

- What was important for you to change?

- "Almost everything. I tried my best to give my child respect even when I did not like what he did. I made sure he was safe and that he knew not to let anyone abuse him. I encouraged him and cuddled him and read him stories and spent time pursuing his interests."

- What did you do to become a better parent?

- "I read every book that I could get my hands on; I went to therapy, and I talked to my friend's parents and watched people with their kids."

- "I took parenting classes and read books on parenting. I tried to imitate people who I thought were good parents. I tried to love and respect myself so that I would be a good example."

Questionnaire: What You Want to Do Differently Than Your Parents

1. What are some of the good things that you learned from either of your parents?

2. In a nutshell, what did your parents do that has negatively affected your life?

3. How do you wish your parents would have treated you? Fill in the blank: "If they loved me, they would have _____."

RANDOM PARENTING ADVICE

4. What was important for you to change when you became a parent?

5. What did you do to become a better parent?

6. Share a story where you had a parenting success, doing the opposite of what your parent(s) would have done.

Building Self-Esteem and Confidence

As a parent you're responsible for helping your child to build their self-esteem. The trick is to find the balance between providing real encouragement, letting them find their way and redirecting them when needed. You can't have them think that everything they do is wonderful. Of course, it's not. The key word here is real. Just be real.

You can't expect yourself to be perfect at everything you try, we all have different gifts. The main thing is to keep trying. Kids should be exposed to different activities to find out what they're good at.

Consider this scenario: You've just told your kids you've signed them up for soccer and it will be fun, fun, fun. Maybe you were a soccer star and you expect your children to be exceptional too. You can encourage them to practice and give them the benefit of your expertise. Maybe they won't catch on like you want them to. Tell them that no one is great at anything when they first try. It takes practice.

Remember that this is about helping them find their strengths. Is it more important for you to be right about the techniques or for them to be OK with themselves? Try to be patient.

As the children grow up and have more experiences, their needs for guidance change. You can build their confidence by letting them make more decisions for themselves. Let your kids gain independence and earn more freedom.

Approach talking to your kids with an open heart and a goal of understanding. Being curious about their point of view can create openness between you. Asking them, "What do you think?", then listening to their response, can give them confidence to make decisions for themselves.

RANDOM PARENTING ADVICE

When kids get a little older, they're bombarded with information at school and from many sources, so you're not their only input. They should be forming their own ideas and feelings about things they are exposed to. By being open to their ideas and listening, you might even learn something from them.

Kids will learn about confidence from watching how you act. While working on being kinder to yourself you can practice saying positive statements. Instead of calling yourself an idiot when you make a mistake, try saying "Oh, silly me..."

If you have low self-esteem you will need to be especially mindful of comments you make about your body image.

When your kids hear you call yourself fat and ugly, they may wonder if they're ugly too. If you're dressing, try saying something positive (or at least not damning) about the experience. "Hmm, these pants don't seem to fit me anymore. Well, they must have shrunk in the wash. Haha. Maybe I'm supposed to get myself some new ones that do fit." "I don't like the way these tan pants look, I feel much better in darker colors. These go in the giveaway pile."

How do those statements sound compared to "Ugh, I'm disgusting! Nothing fits me anymore. I've got to lose weight." Or "Oh, just look at my cellulite through these tan pants. Gross."

It's especially important to model good self-talk for little girls. They'll be bombarded with images of how pretty they are supposed to be. Little boys are listening and forming ideas about how women are supposed to look and feel by hearing you talk about your body image too.

Allowance

Parents can decide when to give allowance and what for. I chose the idea that allowance is given every week to teach kids how to manage money. They can save or spend it and won't need to ask you for everything they want to buy. For us, it didn't depend on whether or not they did their chores.

Chores are part of living in a household, you do them to contribute to the family. I never paid my kids for doing their regular chores like dishes, laundry and cleaning their rooms. They could earn extra money by washing the car or helping with yardwork.

Having their own money gives kids a sense of its limits and value. If you continue to give and always make the choices about what they can buy, they won't learn this valuable lesson. They can learn that you must save up for expensive things. They also learn that items aren't free. That's why we all work.

You can teach them the difference between wants and needs. You'll take care of their needs but not all of their wants. Let's say they get $10 a week starting at age 11. You still pay for the movies and popcorn, but they have money if they want to get candy.

If they want a certain toy, video game or clothing that you don't think is necessary, they can learn to save up for it. This will teach them better than any lecture how valuable money is and how fast it disappears.

They might learn to be more discerning in what they covet. You may one day hear the magical words "Nah, I don't need a new one, mine is just fine".

I appreciate that my kids are grateful for what they have. They learned at an early age that they couldn't have everything they wanted. They knew that they were fortunate to have a lot that others in the world (and even in their school) did not have. They didn't feel deprived if they didn't get the latest, greatest technology.

I wanted my kids to be wise consumers. I never wanted them to struggle with debt problems. One lesson was to be skeptical of commercials. When a toy that my son owned was advertised on TV, I asked Devin, "There's your toy. It looks so cool on TV. Does it really do that? Does it fly through the air and make explosion sounds?" He said "No, it doesn't. I have to use my imagination for that."

I was pointing out that the commercials oversell what their products do, making it seem much more fun than the reality. My hope was for him to think about the truth vs. advertising.

It's hard to have a balance in today's world. It seems especially important for teens to fit in and have things that their friends have. But you can decide what lessons you teach them about material wants and needs.

Children won't remember whether they got the toy they wanted at Christmas 2016, but they will remember flying a kite with you on vacation.

Chores and Responsibility

Realize that your child is growing and capable to help more as they get older. Try to engage your child in the process to get things done around the house. Delegate duties.

Let's say your 10-year-old doesn't clean their room at all without a big fight. You usually end up going in there when she's at school, cleaning and then scolding her with sarcasm later. "Oh, by the way, I enjoyed cleaning your room today."

Sarcasm doesn't work with kids. They tend to be literal, and so it's totally lost on them. It can be very confusing to kids when you say the opposite of what you mean – try not to do it. Your messy daughter will just hear that you enjoyed cleaning her room, she's off the hook and you'll probably do it from now on. The message you were trying to convey is that you wanted her to clean her room before you felt the mess was getting too high and had to intervene.

You could make a chore chart that's easy to follow with age appropriate consequences when chores aren't completed. Instead of shaming and blaming her for being a slob, try thinking about what your goal is. Is it to make her feel like a piggy or to get her to remember to clean her room without asking her?

So, with your true goal in mind, you go to her room to talk to her. Remember that you are talking to a child. Remain calm and sit down.

"Hi sweetie. Oh, your room looks so nice with everything picked up, doesn't it?" No sarcasm please. You want her to agree that it's better with organization and floor space.

"I'm tired of telling you to keep it clean and I bet you don't like it either. What do you think you would be willing to do to keep it clean? What do you need from me to help?" She will probably look like a deer in the headlights because you are being so reasonable and may not be able to come up with any suggestions.

You're the adult who came armed with a plan, "What if we pick out some baskets and shelves to organize your stuff better? We could put a hook on your door for towels and stuff, what do you think?". "I want to help you remember, how about if we make a checklist and put it on your desk/corkboard?" I bet she will agree to this reasonable request and look forward to less conflict about her room.

RANDOM PARENTING ADVICE

You can't stop there. You're setting her up for failure if you just expect the new system to fall into place. Remember she's in training. It's going to take both of you checking and reminding for a few weeks. Remember to look for the positives and not just what's wrong. Is it worth it? I think you'll see that it is.

It will be worth not having to have that fight all the time. You'll also have grown closer by showing her that you're on the same team and that conflicts can be brainstormed into a solution that makes everybody happy. Isn't that a nice life skill?

As your kids get older, they can manage more things and should be expected to take on more responsibility. They don't reach the magical age of 18 and become suddenly ready to take care of themselves. Raising kids is a process that you guide along the way.

I liked to use birthdays to make it exciting that they had reached a new milestone. They can learn to do something else for themselves or to help the household. "Yay! You're 5 now. You can learn to make up your bed. Come on, I'll show you how." Don't worry how well they do it, give encouragement for every attempt they make that gets closer to your goal. Taking care of themselves and helping with chores gives kids a sense of accomplishment and confidence.

Think of things that they can learn to do at each new stage. Make sure you give guidance but try not to discourage their meager first attempts. "Hey, good try. You almost got the water in the dog's bowl. Let me get you a cup with a spout to make it easier."

When my kids each reached the age of 10, I showed them how to start doing their own laundry. There are many steps to getting clean clothes and kids should learn it isn't by magic. I showed them how to measure detergent and turn on the washer. Then, each and every time, reminded them to transfer it to the dryer. They learned the buzzer meant clothes were dry and we would often fold it together. I didn't mind guiding and reminding them each week because I wanted to empower them to learn this life skill.

I'm quite sure I helped with some stage of laundry for the first couple of years, but they would always get it started and put it away. By the age of 12, they were good at doing it all the way through. Even when my kids were 18 and at home, I would still tell them, "the washer's done." But that's OK, everyone needs reminding and I was the observant one.

I wanted my kids to be self-sufficient for their own good and so they wouldn't have to rely on anyone else to do what they were perfectly capable of doing themselves.

It's my philosophy that parenting is a temporary job that we're thrown into to create fully functioning adults. My role as a parent has always been to bring two more happy, contributing members of society into the world.

Parenting is not about keeping your kids dependent on you for everything. It's not empowering to treat them as if they can't do things for themselves. That's called being an enabler. Enabling means to do for another things that they could do for themselves.

Kids can keep track of their homework, wake up to an alarm, catch the bus, go to bed on time, do household chores, be responsible for pets, and much more. However, you can't expect them just to know how to do these things. That's where parenting comes in.

No matter how independent your kids are, they do need you to protect them. The following chapter has advice on ways to keep them safe from harm.

Chapter 7
Child Safety

The biggest worry for parents is for their kid's safety. Even my parents were over-protective and my mother warned us of "bad people" who might hurt us. She made it sound like men wearing black were hiding in the bushes and would jump out and steal us. But she couldn't admit that our beloved father might be the one to betray our trust and hurt us at home.

It was vital for me to protect my children from harm so they would never have to suffer as I had.

I worried about them falling and breaking a bone on the playground, being harassed by a bully or having someone older take advantage of their innocence and hurt them. My job was to protect them to the best of my ability and then to help pick up the pieces when they did get hurt. It's unrealistic that they won't ever get injured, but you want to keep it to a minimum.

As a parent you can be your child's hero. You must take charge and protect them. Here's your chance to stand up and be assertive where their safety is concerned. Don't be afraid to question any other adult where your child's welfare is involved.

Question, Question, Question.

Ask if there are guns in your neighbor's house before you let your kids play there. Question anything you don't understand at the pediatrician's office. Talk with their teacher to gain understanding about any issues at school. Ask your in-home daycare about any other adults that would be around your child.

When neighborhood kids were playing at my house and their parent knocked on the door, I told them to just come in. If their kids were there, they had every right to walk right in – because there wouldn't be any reason for privacy.

One way I protected my children was to communicate with their friends' parents. I was not afraid to check in to make sure of the plans being made. It's very important to know your kid's friends, where they live and who their parents are. It's especially vital when they're teenagers.

When your kids are young and under your supervision you can feel pretty secure about their safety. It gets harder when you must let them go out into the world without you. Make sure they're armed with a sense of their own rights so that no one can take advantage of them.

If you have taught them from an early age that they matter and have a right to their feelings, they will be more likely to know intuitively when they are entering an unsafe situation.

1 in 4 females and 1 in 6 males are sexually abused before the age of 18

You must talk openly about safety issues with your child. Even the uncomfortable ones like kidnapping and molestation. On their level, of course. There are many books to help with these discussions. Using the correct names for private parts is important in case anyone else talks to them using a euphemism. Someone says, "Pet my puppy" and

CHILD SAFETY

Junior can say "Eww. Why do you have your penis out of your pants?" and knows to get away to safety.

Teach your children they have people in their life they can trust and help them to identify who they are. Work together to make a list of teachers, family or neighbors that they could go to for help if they need it. It builds security for them to know that they have "Trusted Adults" that will help them in any situation. There may be times in their childhood when they have problems they don't want to tell their parents.

We want them to know they have a voice to get help when they need it. A way to teach them to trust their instincts is by allowing them to be reluctant to hug and kiss everyone they meet. I believe expecting them to do this is ridiculous behavior. Do you want to hug and kiss everyone you know at every encounter? Hopefully you have boundaries that allow you to hug who you really want to.

Some cultures have a tradition of affectionate greetings and that is, of course, a matter of choice. But it's worth exploring what it teaches children about personal boundaries. It's important to think about it from a little kid's perspective. If you say, "Go on and kiss Uncle Eddie now." This gives them no choice if their little tummy says "yuck, he's hairy and smells funny." They learn to override their feelings in order to please someone else.

I try to let kids greet me however they choose. "Do you want to give me a hug? Not right now? OK that's fine, how about a high five?" Kids don't need to take care of adults' feelings. If Uncle Eddie gets offended, so what? It can be explained to him that you're practicing empowering your child for their safety.

Teaching your children they have choices about their personal space will pay off if they ever encounter someone who wants to overpower them and hurt them.

Hopefully they get a signal from their gut about someone long before they're ever close to being alone with them. In fact, if they learn to trust their gut, they will try to make sure they are never alone with anyone suspicious.

It doesn't matter if Uncle Eddie is the nicest guy in the world and you are (pretty) sure that he wouldn't harm a fly, **let your kid have final say so about giving out their affections.**

Kid Empowerment Can Stop Child Molesters

You can warn your kids against "Stranger Danger" and people who may want to hurt them, but the truth is that child molesters rarely seem like the big, bad boogeyman at first. Child molesters purposely establish a role in a child's life; sometimes in the form of a relative, coach, priest, neighbor, or teacher. They gain their trust and then betray them in the most confusing and unbelievable way.

Of course, not all people who are nice to our children want to harm them. Most people who work with children and enjoy being around them are not perverts, but sometimes it's difficult to tell until it's too late. So how do we protect the kids from this very hidden danger?

Parents need to empower their children to trust their gut and give them permission to go against authority if they feel something is "off". This takes a shift in thinking.

By forcing a child to show physical affection, this robs them of their ability to trust their own feelings. It also makes them feel obligated to have physical contact, as if they have no choice in the matter.

For example: If a child is reluctant to give affection a mother should not say, "She's just shy. Go ahead, honey, give Uncle a hug and a kiss, we've got to go."

CHILD SAFETY

Instead she could say "OK we're leaving. Sally, say bye-bye to everyone. Blow a kiss to Uncle." It gives the child a way out.

A parent could empower their child even more by offering a choice, "Sally, want to give Uncle a hug, high-five or blow him a kiss?" In this scenario, the parent is letting the child know it's OK either way. This is an important lesson that will resonate with a child throughout the teenage years and beyond. Teaching that it's a person's right to set boundaries with others is a valuable life lesson.

As a parent, you might think it's silly when a child balks at hugging and kissing their grandmother. Allow your child to feel whatever they feel. Adults should never be offended if a child doesn't want to hug or kiss them. They certainly shouldn't make the child feel bad about it.

It's my experience that it's not always innocent when a relative pulls a child into their lap. Innocent affection can become part of the grooming process to get close to them. You must be mindful of anyone who is alone with your child.

This is a big shift in behavior for a lot of families. I believe everyone who has contact with children should adopt this mindset. What's more important? Keeping a tradition or challenging that tradition to teach children safe boundaries?

If we could just change this one thing with our small children, it could make a huge difference in their sense of self.

Teach Children to Trust Their Tummy

Intuitive feelings are there to warn us and protect us from harmful situations. If kids are taught to listen to their gut, that it's OK to go with that uneasy feeling, they'll have the ability to protect themselves when their parents are not around.

Like my mother, parents often consistently use mantras like: "Don't talk to strangers", "Never get in anyone's car that you don't know", "Don't let anyone touch you in your private parts". While these are good rules, they are scenarios that children won't encounter as often as day to day choices over their bodies. Giving them real life situations that allow them to choose how comfortable they are with physical affection is a much more powerful tool.

Children will learn to trust their own judgement. Mommy and Daddy don't have to tell them who's OK and who's not. Teaching children to value their own feelings is one of the most empowering tools a parent can give.

Teaching kids that their feelings are just as important as everyone else's is powerful stuff. Especially for little girls who are often taught to "be nice" above all else and to value others' feelings over their own.

As girls grow up, they may find it hard to say "No" when they really want to, which is dangerous. As parents, we're not making our children into monsters by giving them the choice over their own bodies.

Secrets

There's a difference between secrets and surprises. One is supposed to never be told while the other is going to be happily told. Kids need to have it explained to them that keeping secrets can be dangerous. Tell them there's always someone you can talk to about anything. Kids need to have trusted adults that they feel safe to talk to.

Kids may keep secrets between themselves. I know that my sister and I kept lots from our parents. But an adult should never have a secret with a child. There just isn't any reason for it. Like I said in the Honesty chapter, even "white lies" that you ask a child not to tell are tearing down trust. It's not necessary to ask a kid for help in keeping a secret.

Any secret that makes a child feel funny keeping, needs to be told right away to a trusted adult.

Why do Adults Hurt Children?

Understanding why adults hurt children is something I have struggled with. There's supposed to be a family bond that makes humans take care of each other and nurture their offspring to their best ability. But what fails and why do some parents turn against their children and terrorize them?

Sometimes it's because of obvious mental illness – which may or may not be genetic. Some is learned behavior – continuing a cycle of abusive patterns that are passed down through generations.

I've pondered why some people will let themselves commit heinous crimes against children. It just doesn't make sense. How can they rationalize and make it OK to harm a child who depends on them – or at least depends on them not to be abusive?

Children deserve to be treated well and as the precious beings that they are. OK, they don't always act precious and are sometimes downright obnoxious. But that doesn't excuse or invite anyone to beat them or take advantage of them at any time.

I taught my kids to be protective of themselves and their belongings. To be aware of their surroundings and to stay with their friends.

I taught that you must not present opportunities for crime. Although it's not your fault if something happens to you even when you are cautious. Being observant of your surroundings and not putting up the temptation is just being proactive.

So, you don't leave your wallet in plain sight in your car – this could attract someone's' interest that had no intention of breaking into your car – but sees the temptation and "can't help themselves".

I think that warped minds will give themselves permission to do what they crave when an opportunity is in front of them. They rationalize that it's meant for them to do it. A pervert sitting in a park may have had no thought of kidnapping a child until they see one crying and alone.

Parents need to be mindful of potentially bad situations; either watching over their child or teaching them to be on the lookout, depending on the child's age. It's impossible to anticipate all harm but it's important not to be overly trusting that the kids will be fine.

Don't let them walk to the store alone, go with them. Don't leave them on the playground while you jog around the lake, ask another parent that you know to watch them.

Let's say your older child is ready for some independence and to walk to the store alone, how do you teach them to be safe? I believe there's safety in numbers. So, depending on how far away the store is and how old the child is, I still feel that they should go with someone. Of course, it's up to you to determine what your child is capable of handling.

CHILD SAFETY

Before sending my child on a walk alone they would know not to approach anyone in a car who may talk to them, don't deviate from the plan, to check in on their phone and to make a loud fuss if anyone grabbed them. I taught my kids to yell repeatedly, "You're not my mommy (or daddy)" if anyone tried to take them in a public place. I think it's more attention grabbing than "Help."

I don't agree that it's much more unsafe for kids these days, we just have more information about abuse and molestation. You hear about it more often. I do believe it was easier for adults in the past to take advantage and hurt children because no one was talking about it. Now there are weekly news stories about child abuse. People can dismiss these stories as close by, but not really close to them.

While talking about this book and my childhood sexual abuse, I find many people are struck with disbelief that this happens as much as it does. If it wasn't your experience, it's hard to fathom the possibility. It's unthinkable and horrific to contemplate. Our brains want to dismiss the thought immediately. I understand. This is how the subject stays in the dark.

Think about how relatively recently women have had rights as citizens. Only one hundred years ago in 1920, women got the right to vote in America. They were considered property of their fathers and husbands in the past. Children have always been even lower on the human rights scale.

It's always been possible to do whatever you want to family in your own home. In recent years abusers must be more careful to hide the marks. Teachers have a mandate to report any suspected abuse.

The most shocking statistic to me was what I found on the RAINN.org website about parental sex abusers. According to a 2016 report by Child Protective Services, US Dept. of Health and Human Services: Out of 63,000 reported sexual child abuse cases that year, **80% of the perpetrators were a parent**.

My case is not unique, unfortunately.

Children may be taught to act like nothing's wrong but there are usually signs of abuse. Notice if they withdraw or seem angry. Say something if your partner does anything you think is inappropriate. What if they still think it's fine to take showers with your 9 or 10 year-old? Can you speak up if your partner sleeps naked with your child in bed?

Do you feel safe to approach your partner with your views? Can you calmly discuss your growing child's needs for privacy? If you are afraid that they will be mad and call you crazy, it's a red flag.

If you have any suspicion that your child has been abused, you must investigate. You must take action to make the abuse stop. Don't be like my mother and hide your head in the sand. Be brave and ask questions. Do what you need to do to protect your child and to get them help.

If you suspect any child of being abused you can anonymously report it to police or child protective agencies. There are probably reporting agencies in your area, like the Department of Children and Family Services.

Go to the **RAINN.org** website to find all kinds of topics on the subject. In their "Safety and Prevention" section there's information for parents, students, what consent looks like, warning signs, and how to talk to your kids about a range of safety issues.

While you must protect your kids as much as possible, it's important to prepare your children to take care of themselves. As they get older, they need to be empowered to assess unsafe situations and people. The next chapter will

CHILD SAFETY

discover the joy of having teenagers – and yes, there are moments of joy.

Chapter 8

Dealing with Teenagers

What are the two things that all toddlers and teenagers need? To be heard and understood. Who can understand a teenager? Other teenagers. That's why they flock together and think the rest of the world is stupid and clueless.

Teenagers speak their own language and don't think they need to hear from you at this point in their lives. They'll come to you when they need something. Usually it will be for permission to go somewhere, take the car and for more money. This doesn't mean that you abandon them or leave them to their own devices. Quite the contrary, you'll need to be aware of what's going on from a distance.

Don't lose track of your teen just because they may be pushing you away. Realize that it's normal for them to want a lot of time alone in their room. Check on them occasionally (always knocking first) and let them know that you notice they aren't around.

"Hey, you want to come out and watch the game with me at 4:00?" Even though you may get a "no" answer, it goes into their brain that you care. Plus, everyone wants to be invited to something. Invite them to participate in family dinner, movie night, walking the dog, etc.... but don't expect too much.

Teenagers have hormones surging through their bodies causing feelings that they can't understand or express well, and it's sometimes best for them to be left alone. Often, they're feeling angry at the world and you don't need to get in the way.

It's a balance of giving space and letting them know you still care. It's necessary to do both. It can become a habit for them to walk straight to their hideout, barely speaking to the rest of the family and disappear for hours at a time. They're sending a signal that they don't want to be approached or questioned. But I believe a parent still needs to check in and ask a few questions about their life to let them know they care.

It's hard to put forth invitations or questions that you know will probably be met with a one-word grunt, but the message is that you're still there in their life and will be there when they become human again. It will happen.

The hardest thing for me was not taking it personally when my kids turned into teens and started shutting me out. We had always been so close and then they didn't want to talk to me or let me know why they looked so sad or mad. Guess what? They probably didn't know why they felt that way. Also, it probably had something to do with one of their friends, was private and they didn't want to share.

The teen years are a natural time of pulling away from parents in order to figure out how to deal with life without you. It's nature's way to make them obnoxious and hard to reach so that you can let them go. Don't take it personally. You really don't want your kids attached to you when they're 30.

But what do you do when they say, "I hate you!" I guess it's a rite of passage for teens at some point. My angel children each said it to me one time as I recall. My reaction must've been what stopped them from ever doing it again.

DEALING WITH TEENAGERS

I was already in teenager-mom mode where I didn't take their actions too personally when they got mad at me. I had probably restricted them from doing something that was so important to their whole life (or at least that weekend).

"I hate you." was spat out of my little darling's mouth as she slammed her bedroom door. I took a deep breath and followed with a knock and a walk in "Sierra, I know that you are very disappointed, and I am very angry with you right now too. But it's unacceptable for you to say that you hate me, I know it isn't true. I love you and I know you love me." Walk away, enough said.

Here's where that skill of naming their feelings and yours comes back into play. Teenagers are raging with feelings that they can't control. They may seem bi-polar at times.

Try not to get caught up in the whirling river. Let it swirl around you while you are the rock. You will be there when these days of rapids pass by. There will be calm pools of water where you can soak up the return of your loved one before they hurdle down another rapid.

Relish the times when you see your happy, talkative teenager reappear. Don't get too giddy and pounce on them with lots of questions. They could get skittish and retreat to their cave. Just enjoy the time with them and give them some compliments. "It's great to see your smile. Good job for doing your homework on your own. That's a great color on you."

It's wonderful to say "Good Job" as often as you possibly can. Too often, teenagers make it difficult to find wonderful things to say about them. Because you only get a glimpse of them each day, you may tend to bark out quick orders about what they need to do or criticize what they haven't done.

"You left your shoes outside all night. Remember it's garbage night. You need to do your laundry today." It's all they expect to hear out of you. Occasionally throw them for a loop and say:

" I like that shirt on you"

"How would you like me to make brownies tonight?"

"Thanks for doing your laundry"

Moms seem to be especially observant of everything in the house and can see when anything is out of place. "Who left the milk out? Who dragged the mud into the house? The good scissors are missing." That's the job apparently. It's part of a survival instinct, we must keep track of the inventory and know when the milk is about to run out. But it can lead you to be hyper-critical which is especially irritating to the teenage brain.

So, here's a challenge: Turn your detective skills toward finding the positive things going on in the house.

"Who brought in the garbage cans?"

"Good job straightening your room."

"I notice you fed the dog."

It doesn't seem natural to look for the good things and may be hard at first, but it's refreshing to recognize that your teenager isn't always lazy and unhelpful.

For me, it hadn't always been natural to look for the good things. My parents certainly hadn't done that. As I remember it, my parents were only critical of me and they didn't have a clue about my life.

Communication is key if you want to keep in touch with your kids. This means asking open-ended questions instead of, "How's school, good?" This is like the store clerk who asks,

"How are you today?" They're not really interested in hearing about your day.

When you're aware of what's going on in their world you can ask, "How did you do on that test today?" "Are you still having challenges in math class?" "Did you get Saturday off from work to go Grandpa's birthday dinner?"

There will be more important subjects to investigate with your teenager too.

Getting Your Teen to Talk

Sometimes you need to give your teenager space not to talk to you about everything. Other times it's critical that you find out what is going on in their life. You're still their protector even if they don't want you to be.

I heard this effective strategy on Oprah Radio to get them to open up when it's really important. If tensions are high, then you can use this practice when you have all calmed and sit down to talk.

Remember that you aren't a prosecutor trying to prove what you already believe. The goal is to try to remain calm and be curious.

Here's the magic formula:

1. Ask: "Is there any reason why..." (You were out so late? Your eyes are red?)
2. "Really?" (Keep it simple. You are trying to give them room to talk)
3. W. A. I. T. (Pause...This stands for Why.Am.I.Talking)

PARENTING WELL AFTER CHILDHOOD ABUSE

4. Calmly use their name "Junior, is there anything you want to get off your chest?"*

   *Nodding your head Yes while asking this.

Your tone needs to convey that you're on their side and want to hear the truth. All of that honesty you fostered when they were younger should come into play here. Ideally, they will come clean and tell you what's going on. If you want to tell if they're lying, ask yourself if their explanation is trying to Convince or Convey.

If they are trying hard to convince (sell) you on their story, then at least parts of it are untrue. If they are conveying information that clarify the story, then it's probably true.

Raising teenagers is harder than ever. They are very distracted by electronic input and the pressures on them are great. Finding a balance of giving them room while showing you care is a worthwhile challenge.

Don't forget that it's normal behavior for them to withdraw and want to be alone. But watch to make sure they aren't withdrawing from friends and activities, losing/gaining weight or showing anxiety. Depression and anxiety, which can lead to drug problems or suicidal thoughts, are on the rise in teenagers.

According to Helpguide.org, 1 in 5 adolescents will experience depression. They suggest parents:

Focus on listening, not lecturing

Be gentle but persistent

Acknowledge their feelings

Trust your gut

DEALING WITH TEENAGERS

You can also encourage your teen to have social connections that are face to face and not just online. Make physical health a priority. Encourage them to eat well and get plenty of sleep. Taking care of themselves will help them to deal with the challenges of being a teenager.

The teenage years can be a roller coaster for everyone in the family. My children may not have always liked my rules and involvement in their lives, but they knew I loved them.

I balanced my goal of being close to my kids with giving them space and freedoms. I worked to not take their attitudes personally and to keep the lines of communication open. This is how I know that it's possible to enjoy – most of – the teenage years.

Conclusion

Now that my kids are out of college, my role as a parent is changing once again as it has many times as they've grown. I now have a feeling of "Yay! They're grown and out of here." It's very exciting because I have every confidence in these fantastic, likeable people. They will be fine.

I have taught them how to take care of themselves, shared my philosophies on life and now it's their time to go out and find their own way. They need to find what speaks to their hearts and follow where life takes them.

I feel good about giving them a good foundation that was full of love, laughter and getting through some tough times too. I wasn't easy on my children, but I hope that they don't think I was too hard.

It's not easy going from being vigilant to take care of their every need, to letting them go little by little as they gain independence. But that's my definition of parenting well.

There's a bittersweet point where you've done your job and it's time for them to go out into the world without you. What you've taught them will stay in their minds for guidance. You will always be there if they need you, but you hope that they are ready to deal with life's challenges.

Parents always worry about their children no matter how old they are. Once they're adults it's a relief to give up the responsibility to take them to the next levels in their lives.

It's been a long and winding road. When I had my daughter, I felt clueless as to how to be a parent. My son came along 3 years later as I was getting the hang of parenting. I had also been in therapy and was healing myself day by day.

I broke the cycles of denial and abuse and I found resources to help me. If you're seeking help, it will come to you. There's a Buddhist saying: "When the student is ready, the teacher will appear."

Your hard work to heal yourself will be worth it. Accepting and loving yourself will get easier. Your children's love will be there to help. They'll remember your acceptance and love for who they turn out to be.

Have fun and don't take yourself so seriously. Don't be afraid to show the dichotomy of being a real person. You must at times be firm and others soft, able to cry and laugh out loud, decisive and then flexible.

Ah, the joys of Parenting! Everyone says it is the hardest job and the most important. I've found that's true. The journey will turn out exactly as it should. Just do your best. Learn new skills and practice, practice, practice.

You are enough. You're a strong survivor. You can heal yourself and raise your children at the same time. It's never too late to live in your truth.

Recommended Reading

Parenting:

Faber, Adele and Mazlish, Elaine. Liberated Parents Liberated Children. New York, New York: Avon Books, 1975

Faber, Adele and Mazlish, Elaine. How to Talk So Kids Will Listen & Listen So Kids Will Talk. New York, New York: Scribner, 2012

Phelan, Thomas W. 1-2-3 Magic, Effective Discipline for Children 2-12. Glen Ellyn, Illinois: ParentMagic, Inc. 2010

Self Help:

Bass, Ellen and Davis, Laura. The Courage to Heal. New York, New York: Harper and Row, 1988

Street, Rebecca. You Can Help. Self-published, 2016

Katie, Byron. Loving What Is: Four Questions That Can Change Your Life. New York, New York: Harmony Books, 2002

Ruiz, Don Miguel. The Four Agreements. San Rafael, California: Amber-Allen Publishing, 1997

Chapman, Gary. The Five Love Languages. Chicago, Illinois: Northfield Publishing, 1995

Resources

RAINN.org – Rape, Abuse & Incest National Network 1800-656-HOPE (4673)

National Suicide Prevention Hotline 1800-273-TALK (8255)

Childhelp, National Child Abuse Hotline 1800-4-A-CHILD (2-24453)

HealWriteNow.com

1in6.org – For male survivors of sexual abuse and assault

Acknowledgements

Many thanks to my friends who gave such unwavering support and belief in my story that it freed me to tell it. I know that I'm a good person because I have so many wonderful friends who love me. You are in my heart; Bonnie, Angie, Terri, Tracey, Sherri and more.

Bonnie's whole crazy family adopted me. Carl and Valerie are my surrogate parents – I adore you and consider you my family.

Speaking of family, this book is only possible because I survived alongside Terrin. She taught me about love and honesty. We have always taken turns being the "strong one."

I'm grateful to my husband, Joel, who has always supported the importance of this book to me. Sierra and Devin are the reasons I worked so hard on parenting well. My heart bursts with gratitude for their presence in the world.

Thank you; Stacie Booker, my friend and editor, whose feedback and cheerleading helped tremendously to make my ideas make more sense. Thanks to Kathyrn V. for final edit.

While I started writing this book in 2012, I let fear and life distractions keep me from completing it. It's only due to the community and support of Chandler Bolt's "Self-Publishing School" that got me to the finish line. Gary Williams, my writing coach, was inspiring and helpful at every speed bump.

I also want to thank Susan Komater, massage therapist extraordinaire. She was my friend, mentor, confidante and upheld me during some of my darkest times. I hope she gets a copy of my book in heaven – from the cloud!

I want to acknowledge all the survivors in the world who bravely tell their stories and work to help other people heal from sexual abuse.

Thanks also to Connie and Shelagh who made the finishing touches:

Photo credit: Love, Constance Photography

Illustrations: Shelagh Leutwiler

About the Author

Geanne Meta is a childhood sexual abuse survivor who isn't afraid to talk about it. She has a passion to share her story in hopes of helping the multitude of others who suffer in silence. Her passion is to help children have better lives and believes helping their parents to heal is the first step.

She has volunteered at the Crisis Center of Tampa Bay and was a member of their Empowerment Group. She spoke at Tampa's Take Back the Night in 2014 and was a contributor with her story at Cup of Compassion in 2015. You can find the link on YouTube.

Even though inappropriate touch caused her pain, Geanne chose massage therapy as a career. She has practiced for over 23 years to provide safe and healing touch to hundreds of happy clients.

Geanne has a son, daughter and "bonus" son by marriage. She is now blessed with a granddaughter and takes delight in seeing her daughter's parenting skills. She enjoys time with her husband camping, kayaking, hiking and exploring the outdoors. They have 2 cats, 2 dogs and live in Florida.

Thanks for reading my book – all the way to the last page!

CAN YOU HELP?

I appreciate your feedback
and would really love to hear what you think.

What inspiration or nugget spoke to you?

Please take a minute to leave an honest review on
Amazon (or wherever you bought the book).

It will help the book to reach more people who may need it.

+ Book Challenge +

Use the hashtag #ParentingWellAfterChildhoodAbuseBook

To share on Twitter, Instagram, Facebook

Thank you so much!

- Geanne Meta

Group Discussion - Individual Work Guide

PART 1 – Healing Yourself

Chapter 1 – Breaking the Cycle of Abuse

1. Do you agree that most people feel "not good enough"? Do you believe that childhood abuse survivors feel this more than others?

2. The author calls children gifts to the earth and parents their caretakers. Do you agree children can be treated as possessions, slaves or reflections of their parents?

3. Why is breaking the cycle of blaming yourself so important? What would it take to believe it wasn't your fault?

4. Do you believe it's necessary to break the cycles of denial, self-blame, anger, shame and negative self-talk to be a whole person? Which one is hardest for you?

Chapter 2 – Why Go to Therapy?

1. Do you agree that you need to get past your adult thinking about the abuse and get to the deep feelings of your inner child to start the healing?

2. Can you relate to reacting to something out of proportion to the current event? These are called triggers. Are you aware of some of your triggers? Do you understand that therapy can help you identify where your intense feelings come from?

3. What parts of the Worksheet to Connect with Your Inner Child seemed most helpful? Most difficult?

Chapter 3 – How to Get Out of Denial

1. In what ways have you or your family members been in denial?

2. Why is it necessary to break out of denial and accept the reality to heal fully? How does denial keep you stuck?

3. How do you think being around her friend, Bonnie's family helped the author? How did you learn about healthier families?

4. Can you understand why the author denied that her mother knew about the abuse and how hurtful it was to find out that she was complicit? Can you relate?

5. When you're in denial you aren't listening to your inner child's voice. In what ways does it try to get your attention?

6. If you take the blame for the abuse you might not believe it can happen to anyone other than you. Why is this dangerous?

Chapter 4 - Boundaries

1. How hard is it to set boundaries with people when you couldn't as a child? With whom have you set healthy boundaries? Where do you struggle with having boundaries?

2. Why is it so hard to set boundaries and do things differently when it comes to your family of origin?

3. How does a need to control others make it hard to accept their boundaries?

Chapter 5 – Learning to be Kind to Yourself

1. "Survivors of child abuse can have low self-esteem, negative thoughts about themselves and feel unworthy of

love." How do these feelings impact your happiness? Why is it important to accept and love yourself?

2. List your accomplishments. Go ahead take a minute and write down anything you have done that you feel good about.

3. Look at yourself as you are today and list attributes that you like about yourself. They can be physical, you have a nice smile; or deeper, you are trustworthy. If you find yourself pausing and having trouble, think about what your best friend (or dog) would list as your good qualities.

4. Make a list of things you can do for self-care. The author suggests affirmations, sticky notes, take a bath, get a massage, give yourself flowers and writing yourself love letters. Do you have trouble putting yourself as a priority?

5. Do you have trouble being present? When do you find yourself tuned out? What are some ways that you can anchor yourself to the present?

Chapter 6 – Relationships and Divorce

1. The author wonders if she was in danger of repeating her distant mother's pattern with her own daughter. Do you think there's a subconscious level of behavior when our children are at the same age as we remember being abused?

GROUP DISCUSSION – INDIVIDUAL WORK GUIDE

2. Do you understand that you need to love and respect yourself to have a healthy, adult relationship? Have you allowed a partner to disrespect you? Do you have a pattern of failed relationships?

3. Why is it important to be honest about your past with a significant partner? Can you trust yourself to pick someone you can be open with?

4. Have you ever felt that your partner is acting like your abuser? Do you see the value in anchoring to the present and trying to break this identification?

5. What did you learn from your parents about marriage and their roles in it? Explore what you believe about your role as father/husband or mother/wife. Is there any reason to change that belief?

6. In conflicts, do you agree that the person who feels most strongly about a subject should get to be the decider about it?

7. Do you relate to having difficulty figuring out your triggers, why you feel stress and asserting your needs in a relationship?

Chapter 7 – Forgiveness

1. Finding some level of forgiveness enables you to move on. Do you believe you have found forgiveness for your abuser? For yourself? Is it necessary?

2. Do you understand how the author found it easier to hate her mother than her father? He was the perpetrator, but she was dependent on him and he gave her attention. Did you have a love/hate relationship with your abuser? Can you forgive yourself for being a needy child?

3. Do you understand that forgiveness is for yourself to find peace and move forward? What are reasons you may not choose to forgive?

PART 2 – Raising Good Kids

Chapter 1 – Children's Bill of Rights

1. Did you have rights as a child? Which of the 6 Rights resonate most with you?

2. How can you remain mindful of treating your children with dignity and respect?

3. What do you think about the author's statement, "People are so used to hearing degrading comments

GROUP DISCUSSION – INDIVIDUAL WORK GUIDE

about females that it's passed over as joking – nobody means anything hurtful. This thinking needs to be challenged. It's harmful – especially to children who are gathering information like sponges"?

Chapter 2 – Honesty is the Best Policy

1. Do you have trouble being honest with others, yourself or your children? Is honesty important to you?

2. Can you see that if your goal is to promote honesty, then you need to let your child's confessions lead to solutions and not punishment? Do you see the value in encouraging children to tell the truth without fear of being in trouble?

Chapter 3 – The Power of Apology

1. Did your parents apologize to you as a child? Were their apologies empty?

2. Do you see the value in saying you're sorry to your children? By showing that you make mistakes it helps them to accept their own humanness. Do you agree?

3. Discuss the differences between a true apology and one that is placing blame.

   "I'm so sorry for how I acted earlier. I shouldn't have yelled and pushed you into your room. I know it scared you and I don't want to hurt you. Can you forgive me?"

Versus: "I'm so sorry for losing it and yelling at you earlier, but you..."

Chapter 4 – Managing Expectations. Accepting Feelings

1. Do you think your parents had low or high expectations of you? Do you remember how that felt?

2. "It's a child's right to act childish." Was it OK for you as a child to be imperfect? Can you allow this to be alright?

3. Can you understand how having low expectations of children hurts their self-esteem? Can you teach that failure is inevitable but it's important they keep trying to improve?

4. Did you get the message that expressing negative feelings was a bad thing? Are you afraid of your own strong feelings? What if you could have felt understood and that all feelings were acceptable?

5. Discuss the differences in accepting feelings of boys vs. girls. Do you understand why girls get the message to "be nice", not to express anger, while boys are told to "man up" and not express sadness? What feelings have you repressed?

GROUP DISCUSSION – INDIVIDUAL WORK GUIDE

6. It's Ok for a child to be upset sometimes. Can you see the value of naming the feeling, acknowledging that they feel it, watching for it to pass and then moving on to problem solving? In the long run isn't this better than rushing them from their reaction to trying to fix it?

7. If you had harsh treatment by a parent, you may want to be your child's best friend and try to keep them happy. Why is this not a good idea?

Chapter 5 – Who's in Charge?

1. Why is it hard for survivors to feel like adults sometimes? Do you realize that you could be tougher or softer on your children?

2. Why is it important to follow up on rules and teach your kids that you mean what you say? Have you learned to "pick your battles?"

3. If you have a partner, do you feel that one of you takes on more of the burden in parenting? Have you examined your beliefs about your roles? Is it acceptable for one to ask for more help?

Chapter 6 – Random Parenting Advice

1. Where have you looked for parenting advice? Do you feel like you are soaking up knowledge because of your parent's poor example?

2. Fill out the Questionnaire: What you Want to Do Differently Than Your Parents. Discuss any answers that you want to share. Is it hard to remember good things from your parent(s)?

3. "Kids will learn about confidence from watching how you act." Are you aware of your negative self-talk around your children? What are some things you call yourself and what are the alternatives?

Chapter 7 – Child Safety

1. Survivors of childhood abuse are very protective of their children. What measures do you take to make sure they are safe?

2. Do you feel able to question doctors, teachers, neighbors and anyone where your child's safety is concerned?

3. What do you think about the idea of letting your kid have final say so about giving out their affections? Can you see how making them obligated to hug and kiss adults teaches them that their feelings don't matter? How do you feel about this?

4. Why is it important to teach children to "trust their tummy?"

GROUP DISCUSSION – INDIVIDUAL WORK GUIDE

5. Discuss whether kids are less safe than in the "old days".

6. According to a 2016 report by Child Protective Services, US Dept. of Health and Human Services: Out of 63,000 reported sexual child abuse cases that year, 80% of the perpetrators were a parent. Does this surprise you?

7. Can you be brave enough to discuss it with your partner if you believe they are doing anything inappropriate around your child?

Chapter 8 – Dealing with Teenagers

1. How can you let your teen know that you care while giving them space? Why is it dangerous to let them isolate themselves completely?

2. Can you see the importance of giving praise and compliments to your teen? They are often full of negativity, which makes it harder.

3. Discuss the struggles of communicating with your teenager. Are there any patterns that you can turn around?

4. Practice role playing the "Magic Formula" to getting teens to talk. Is this practical? Can you see how this could work?

Are you inspired to further heal yourself
and be a better parent for your family?

Can you shed the shame and talk about
your childhood abuse as a survivor?

Can you think of people you know
who can benefit from this book?

If you found this valuable will you share it with others?

www.ingramcontent.com/pod-product-compliance
Lightning Source LLC
Chambersburg PA
CBHW020415080526
44584CB00014B/1341